Through The Storms

Annie M.

A Story of Enduring Hope and Survival in a Life Filled with Pain

Through The Storms

Author: Annie M.

Nissi Publishing, Inc.
Roanoke, TX

The names have been changed to reflect my desire to help people and not dishonor anyone. Also, because I feel that the attributes, character and things of God deserve to be honored and recognized, they have been capitalized.

Printed in the United States of America.

ISBN: 978-0-944372-22-7

Table of Contents

A Word from the Author

I have found that following God throughout my life has been the one thing that has made my life worthwhile. The storms of life have not held me back nor stifled my living for Him. On the contrary, they have taught me more about myself and my relationship with Him. The hardest times have actually been the times when I learned the most and grew the most spiritually. Why? The storms forced me to admit my own weaknesses and lean hard on God. During those difficult times, He taught me with His Wisdom. I could never have learned all the things I needed to know to have a happy, purposeful life without God teaching me and guiding me through the trials and tests. And yet, as bad as the storms were, I would not trade them for any amount of money. They brought me so much closer to God and caused me to learn to love Him so much more.

I believe God knew how much I wanted to know Him and love Him. So He allowed me to experience just the right amount of storms to teach me how to do that. Some people do not realize what God is doing by letting them go through hard times and heartaches. If only they could see what He wants to do in their lives and learn to trust Him during those storms! I truly believe that our attitude during those times decides how the rest of our life will go. If we get mad at God and turn bitter, it hardens our hearts and causes us to live beneath His destiny for us. However, if we live through these storms trusting God, believing He knows best and letting Him be in charge, we can learn so much and grow so much stronger.

Life can be a wonderful journey when you trust God and follow Him. It only gets better as you go. I am so thankful I learned to trust Him many years ago. My story is about learning to trust God more each year and letting Him be my Guide as I walk through the many storms of this life here on earth. The greatest desire of my heart is to be close to my Lord and Savior now and throughout all eternity. I believe that is the destiny He has called me to and where I find total joy and contentment.

I determined this one thing:
Whatever storms I walk through here on earth will only bring me
closer to God because I will always trust Him and listen only
to His voice in every decision of my life. I pray that after
reading this book, you, too, will make that same determination.

Chapter 1

Grandma Knows Best

When I was growing up, my grandmother was my HERO! I loved to listen to her tell stories about herself, and I especially loved to hear her talk about how she found God. When Grandma talked about God, it seemed to me she knew Him very well. In fact, from the glow on her face and the twinkle in her eye, I knew Grandma and God were very close, and she loved Him more than anyone else in the world. I remember wanting to be around her all the time because there was such a spirit of love and peace around her, and it would spill over onto me. I always felt so loved and secure when I was near her. I knew she really loved me and was very proud of me. I'd do anything to please Grandma, and I wanted to grow up to be just like her!

I watched her very carefully, searching for the secret to her relationship with God. *What made her different from other people?* When I stayed with her, I'd wake up in the mornings and see her reading her Bible and talking to God as if He were the love and joy of her life. She looked so happy and peaceful—like she wasn't really here ... like she was somewhere else. I would think to myself, *"That's amazing! How does she do that? Grandma and God must be very close."* Sometimes she even put a chair across from her chair and asked God to sit in it so they could talk. As she talked to God and listened for His answer, it was obvious Grandma really was talking to God, and *He* was talking to *her.* I had no doubt about that; I could feel His Presence.

Grandma never acted like being a Christian was a chore or hard for her. She loved God so much that everything she did for Him and the church was such a joy for her. She wanted to be at church whenever she could get there and was so excited to get to go. I have seen Grandma go to church so tired she could barely walk in the door. As the service would start, she would begin singing, and her face would begin to take on a whole new look. The tiredness would disappear, and she would look so refreshed—like a totally different person. I can still see her looking up as if no one was there except her and God. I think all that mattered to her was what she and God were talking about. I got the feeling she didn't even know I was sitting on the bench beside her. She was somewhere else with just her and God. I could feel it, and it made me feel so good to just sit next to her.

Sometimes, Grandma would have big tears running down her cheeks, and she'd stand up and say something God was telling her. People in the congregation would start crying as she talked. I watched as they would get up and go down front to the altar to get saved because of what Grandma was saying. In fact, God spoke many times through Grandma to people who needed to get right with Him.

The very first time I remember hearing God speak to *me* was when I was riding in the car with Grandma. I was about 15 years old, and she was talking to me about what God wanted me to do after I graduated from high school. I had thought maybe God wanted me to be a missionary. As we were talking, I heard God speaking. He said, *"I don't want you to be out front. You will always be in the background."* I told Grandma I felt God was changing my plans. She was a little surprised but said, "Oh, okay." Since that time, I have tried to obey what God told me that day. I have sensed Him reminding me of it throughout the years. I never take the forefront without asking Him if it's okay. Only once or twice have I felt He gave me permission to do that. I am so glad I had a grandmother who taught me to hear God and always listen for His guidance. It really pays to listen to Him.

Years later, when Grandma's health began to fail, I realized she was not going to be here much longer. I had such a feeling of emptiness inside. I had started walking daily to be alone with God in prayer and to seek Him earnestly. My walks got longer and longer as my relationship with God grew deeper and deeper. It was as if God walked beside me each day. One day, I asked God, "Who will pray for me and my family every day like Grandma did?" I wondered who would carry our burdens to God in prayer. She was my spiritual pillar, and she was so close to God! I continued to walk and talk to God, always asking, "Who will take Grandma's place?" One day, I heard Him answer me very clearly: *"You will."* I was totally shocked! I couldn't take Grandma's place! I was totally inadequate for that job. I made so many excuses until finally I realized God was clearly giving me this new assignment. What an assignment! How could I prepare for this?

I began crying out to God in desperation. I told Him I wanted Him more than anything in this world. I asked Him to please give me the faith and confidence in Him my grandmother had. Then, for some reason I added, "But please God, don't take me through all the heartache Grandma went through." As I spoke those words, I realized then the trials she had gone through had made her what she was. She had learned to lean on God and have faith in Him through every trial, every heartache. He became her closest *Friend*, her *Comforter*, her *Strength* and her *Provider* **because** of her trials. Even though I had hesitated at first, I finally said "Yes" to God's will. I wasn't sure what would be ahead for me, but I knew I truly hungered to be close to God—just like Grandma was.

He became her closest Friend, her Comforter, her Strength and her Provider because of her trials.

Chapter 2

Surviving PTSD

When I was born, my parents lived out in the country in a small farming town. We soon moved to a fairly large city nearby, since my mom and dad both worked there. We moved from house to house when I was small. My parents would remodel a big house and then sell it and make a great deal of money. Then we moved on to another house to remodel. Usually my grandparents would live with us and help with the remodeling. Grandma was very good at wallpapering and taking care of me while my parents worked. Grandpa worked as a railroad switch repairman and spent most of his weeks out of town traveling. That left me and my grandmother home together for most of my young childhood.

When I was five years old, my baby brother, John, was born. I wasn't too sure about having him around at first. I had been an only child and grandchild up to that time. I finally learned to love him, but I sure did hate the fact that he was always sick. Because of him, we had to stay home all the time. He caught everything! He was very sick the first five years of his life—until he got his tonsils out. After that, he was perfectly healthy. The one thing I hated the most about John was that he constantly teased. He was unmerciful with his teasing. Sometimes I thought I'd lose my senses with him. He loved it the most when I got upset. He'd laugh as if to say, "That's what I wanted." He was good to me most of the time, and we got along pretty well, except when he teased me.

I always liked going to church with Grandma until my mother finally started attending church regularly. About the time John was born, my mother became a Christian, and we always went to church together after that. Before that time, my favorite pastime was going to movies with my mom. She was a movie addict! On Saturday afternoons, we bought candy and popcorn and spent the afternoon in the movie theatre—just Mom and me. After she became a Christian, she gave up going to movies because she knew she was addicted to them. Also, our church did not look favorably on going to the movies. I hated that, but at least Mom was taking me to church now. I had begged her to get saved previously. In fact, the night she accepted Christ, I stood next to her sobbing because she wasn't a Christian. I told her I didn't want her to go to hell. She decided she wouldn't and turned her life over to Christ right then.

By the time I was in the third grade, I was going to my fourth school. I hated making new friends. I was very shy. I remember standing by the side of the school building crying because I had no friends. I made very good grades, but I felt very alone and afraid of everyone. About the time I would finally start making friends, we'd move again! It seemed useless. I came to realize my best and longest lasting friends would be at my church. So, at least I could look forward to seeing my church friends on Sundays and Wednesdays.

When I entered the third grade, we moved back to the country. My dad promised me we would stay in that house until I graduated. I could hardly believe it, but he really did keep his promise to me—we never moved again. After moving into that house, it took a few months, but I slowly began to make friends. Then I got pneumonia and almost died, but that actually helped me quite a bit with making friends. It caused me to get the attention of my school teacher and the entire class. They all drew me pictures, and the teacher brought them to me at the hospital. My teacher realized I was having trouble making friends after talking to my mother at the hospital. So, she helped me when I came back to school.

After a year or two, my mother quit work until I was in high school. I felt much more secure. I began to enjoy everything more when Mom was home all the time. Coming home after school to the smell of homemade bread and supper cooking was one of my favorite childhood memories. Having my friends over, running through our sixty-five acre woods and playing on my rope swing overlooking a hill was so much fun! My swing was a big hit with all my friends, too. My mother also started chaperoning my church and school activities. All the kids loved my mom. She was such a fun person to be around. She was always joking and playing. All the kids just loved to have her with us.

So did I. I thought I had the prettiest, most intelligent, most talented and best mom in the world! I loved my mom very much and always admired her for her wit. She said the craziest things to make people laugh.

I also had a very generous father. He loved working hard and helping people. At the age of five, during The Great Depression, his father, William, had disappeared and his mother had a hard time providing for him and his four small siblings.

William's parents were quite wealthy. They owned two businesses in New England, but when their son left, they were not willing to help support their daughter-in-law or their five grandchildren. They were never fond of William's wife, Elise—probably because she was a German immigrant. They didn't want to help her at all, and they actually wanted to put their *own* grandchildren on a train and send them to an orphanage in the South! Elise refused to let them do that. She took her five children and headed to a Midwestern farm where her parents had settled. Her parents were poor but willing to take in their daughter and her children. The children all pitched in and did chores to help their grandfather do his farm work. Grandpa was a hardworking German and expected everyone else to pull their weight too. Sometimes, he could be very stern (to say the least).

All went well for about three years. In the third year, Elise's mother died suddenly, and her father took it extremely hard. He was unable to continue farming without his wife's support. The entire family had to move off the farm. Elise took her children and moved into a house in a very small town, a little south of the farm. They rented the house from a wealthy doctor and his unmarried sister, who was a school teacher. It was such a small town, they only had one doctor for the entire area. His sister taught music and art at the school in town, and everyone knew them well.

Elise started taking in washing to provide food for her family. She was a very hard worker, but she just couldn't make enough to pay rent and buy food for her five children. So my dad's baby sister went back east to stay with their aunt who had asked if she could raise her. That still left four mouths to feed. My dad felt the need to work and provide his own keep at the young age of eight, so he went up to the doctor's house, knocked on the door and offered to take care of the yard (which took up a whole city block) if they'd let him live with them. The doctor and his sister really liked my dad, so they agreed to let him live with them and take care of the yard. Before long, they asked if they could adopt my dad, but my grandmother would not sign over her rights as his mother.

So, from then on, my dad had two families: his biological mother and four siblings and the doctor and his sister. This new home was much different from his previous home. He had to eat with silver, china, cloth napkins, lots of silverware, and he had to learn proper manners—how to talk, what to say and what not to say. The doctor and his sister were not emotional people, but they did take very good care of my dad, and it was obvious they loved him very much. He never wanted for anything materially from then on. In fact, he was embarrassed because he had better clothes than any of the other kids in town. He had the best of everything from age eight to seventeen when he joined the Army and went to fight in WWII.

My dad talked often to us kids about how hard his mom and siblings had it after his dad left. I could tell the family probably never did forgive their dad for leaving during a time when food and money were so scarce. "Dad" was a closed subject at family gatherings. In the few times I did hear my dad refer to his own father, I could feel the hurt and hear the anger in his voice.

I believe my dad always loved helping other people so much because he remembered those hard times. During the summertime, my dad raised a huge garden on our farm. He would pack our trunk full of food from our garden. We would go to church and after church was over, Dad would open up our trunk and give away all the food to people in our church who needed it. That was exciting to me as a child!

Mom had to keep an eye on Dad at church during the offering time. If she didn't, he'd put more in the church offering than we could afford to give. He *loved* giving! Mom did, too, but my dad would give away things we really needed. Mom was always telling him to wait and think before he gave things away.

Dad worked hard in our gardens as well as mowing our large country yard. I worked right alongside him. We also mowed the yards for his foster mother and two other older ladies who lived in town. They liked my dad's work and wouldn't let anyone else touch their yards. It was a lot of mowing! I've never known anyone who worked harder than my dad. He was up at 5:00 a.m. and worked nonstop until dark.

I thought my dad was a very good man, and I loved him very much. He didn't become a Christian until I was a sophomore in high school, but he always had a big heart and helped many, many people in any way he could.

When I was 11 years old, my youngest brother was born. My mom and dad had promised me a baby sister if I'd help my mom around the house all summer. Then in the fall, my dad came home to announce I had a new baby *brother!* I said, "A brother! I worked all summer for a baby sister!" Dad saw how upset I was, so he told me he and mom had decided to reward me for all my work by letting me name my brother. That helped my disappointment somewhat. I decided to name him after my dad and my foster grandparents. I named him Matthew after my dad and gave him the doctor and his sister's last name for his middle name. It sounded very professional to me. I hoped he might also become a doctor someday. Mom and Dad agreed on the name, so I felt like I was an important part of my baby brother's life. Being 11, I got to feed him, change him and help teach him a lot of things. It was kind of fun having a baby around. By then, my other brother was five. He was almost ready for school. Mom's pregnancy had allowed her to be able to stay home a lot. Now that she had a baby to take care of, she'd be staying home even more. That meant a lot to me.

My mother had a major issue she dealt with—she had a terrible inferiority complex. Because of that, she never allowed me to invite *school* friends over to my house, no matter how many times they invited me to theirs. I could only have *church* friends over to my house. So, church friends, of course, became my closest friends because I spent more time with them. I never felt bad about having no school friends over because my mom said our house wasn't big enough. She also said they wouldn't like our house. I believed her, but

I still liked our house. I guess I never really thought it through until I was older. My mother was just not comfortable having kids over if she didn't know their parents. She believed everybody was better off financially than we were. It wasn't true, but it was what she believed. She knew our church families and was not intimidated by them.

My mother, like my dad, had also had a tough life when she was growing up. She had so many insecurities because of things that had happened to her. My mother was born seven months after her parents were married. In those times, the 1920's, that was a shameful thing. That caused my mother to feel unwanted because she thought she was an embarrassment to her parents. Also, she lost her two-year-old baby sister when she was about six. She had so many feelings of guilt over that. I think she misunderstood what had happened but never could get over it. She had also been molested several times by her father, but she didn't think her mother would believe her so she kept it to herself. Her father also tried to molest several of her friends when they came to visit. That was such a horrible embarrassment to her! All of these things Satan used to try to defeat my mother and stop her from being the blessing she could have been. I watched my mom and wondered why she said and did certain things that would hurt other people. I think she was just protecting herself. She didn't know God could heal her childhood wounds and set her free from all the pain.

My mother was extremely critical of everyone. As we rode home from church each week, we had to listen to a whole 20 minutes of criticism about everyone in the church from the preacher and the singer to the lady who gave her testimony. My mom criticized their clothes, their English, why they said what they said and how hypocritical they were. Besides being critical, my mom expected perfection. I could hear all this criticism, and I became terribly afraid to do anything in public. I was extremely afraid of making a mistake and having everyone criticize me like my mother did.

I took piano lessons for many years but was terrified to play on stage in my piano recitals. My mind would go totally blank when I saw all the people in the audience. No matter how well I'd memorized my piece, I couldn't play it. I can also remember bringing home my report card with all A's and only one B.

The only comment would be, "What happened here?" Most of the time, I felt very stupid and was afraid to answer questions or ask questions in class. I was afraid the kids would laugh at my stupidity. I even tried to memorize parts of the text books so I could get an A. I didn't trust my own interpretation of what the book said.

During high school, I passed out one day in the lunchroom. I was taken to the hospital, and the doctor said it was easy to see what was wrong. I had a "nervous collapse" after semester tests. I was screaming out in my sleep, "I made an A!" I was placed on sedatives for the rest of that school year. Even though I graduated from high school with a 94 grade point average, I was ashamed I hadn't done better. I see now I had nothing to be ashamed of, but at the time, I didn't know that.

My father had served overseas in WWII for 36 months. He was always in the heat of the battle, and he came home with his nervous system totally destroyed. I could see his hands shaking much of the time, and I could hear his voice shaking often when he talked. He was never diagnosed, but he had what we now know as PTSD (Post Traumatic Stress Disorder). When something happened that would upset him, he would lose complete control of himself.

Many times, when my dad would lose control, he would start screaming and beating us kids. One time, I fell off of my chair at the kitchen table, and he got so nervous he jumped up and grabbed me and started hitting me. Of course, that only made it worse, but he couldn't think clearly when he got upset. He didn't even know what he was doing. My dad beat me and my brothers anytime he became very nervous.

Because of my dad's nerve problems, my home life was not always easy to deal with. I didn't fully understand what caused it, but I knew I wanted to stay away from him when he was nervous. I was especially afraid when my mother went somewhere and left me at home with him. I knew he was always upset when Mom wasn't home, so I usually tried to stay in my room or somewhere he wouldn't notice me. Because of my dad's PTSD, I lived most of my childhood totally traumatized. I can remember crying a lot and even shaking because I was so afraid of everything. I was especially afraid of men—even after I grew up. If a man raised his voice, I shriveled up and tried to get out of his way. That feeling of helplessness kept me in a constant attitude of fear.

I knew my mother and father both loved me very much, so it was easy for me to overlook any shortcomings they had. Even though my mom and dad had trouble saying, "I love you," I just knew they did. Sometimes after my dad would do something that hurt me, my mother would say, "You know he loves you, don't you?" So, that always confirmed to me I was loved, no matter what happened. It was only later as an adult I realized my father really needed help in handling his nerve problems. During those days, we didn't talk about it. That was the only answer we knew. People outside our family never knew my dad had this problem where he lost total control of himself, unless they had seen it for themselves.

Later, when I was a new mother, I struggled over and over with losing my own temper and acting like my dad had acted. I would start to lose control and scream and whip my oldest son for small insignificant little things. As I tried to understand why, I realized I was mimicking my father. I was doing the one thing to my child that had hurt me the most—and the one thing I had hated the most. *How could I do this? Had I learned this from my dad? Why was it so inherent in me to do this?*

I knew it was wrong, and I determined not to treat my child as I had been treated. After much prayer and determination, I overcame the PTSD that had been passed down to me. That was the first time I realized how important it is to be freed from the bondages that are passed down generationally. I had never heard of anything like that before. I just knew I surely didn't want to pass that fear or generational curse onto my children. With God's help, I knew I could be set free from this terrible reaction.

It wasn't until I was about 45 years of age that I realized I had actually endured a great deal of "abuse" as a child! That was why I was so afraid of men and criticism. Though my parents had done their best raising me, they had passed down some terrible bondages/curses *(habits or actions)* to me. About that same time, I was learning how bondage could hold you back spiritually. After much prayer and understanding of what was wrong with me, I began to be healed of many deep wounds and to have a new type of freedom I had never thought possible. Letting God come in and heal my childhood wounds was such a wonderful experience.

I also began to see how God had actually used the abuse and criticism to bring me so much closer to Him. I clung to God dearly when I was afraid and overcome by fear because I *knew* He loved me. I knew I wanted to be close to Him where I felt love and peace. I had seen that great peace and love of God in my grandmother's life so clearly. I truly believe had I not known about God and had I not had such a great faith in Him, I would not have found my way in this life. I don't know where I'd be today.

Freedom from the bondages Satan uses to hold us back is a lifelong challenge. I will continue to ask God to heal me and free me as long as I am on this earth. He is the great *Deliverer* if we just ask Him.

Letting God come
in and heal
my childhood
wounds was such
a wonderful
experience.

Chapter 3

Dating Merry-Go-Round

As a child, I knew I would marry a Christian man. There was never any doubt I wanted a Christian home when I grew up. I wanted to serve God the best I knew how and raise a Christian family. In fact, that was the only dream I had for my future. I had no desire to have any other career. Much to my parent's dismay, being a wife and mother was my life's ambition.

The church we attended was a conservative church. There were several guys I became friends with there, but one seemed to be quite different than the others. A guy named Danny seemed to be very serious about God and the Bible. He took everything the preacher said very seriously, and he always listened during church services. I observed him very carefully when we were teenagers. He became President of Youth for Christ at his high school of about 2500 students, Vice President of our local Youth Society, a singer in a gospel quartet, and he won District Speech Contests. He was even asked to give the benediction at his Senior Class Baccalaureate Service when he was graduating from high school—out of 600 graduates. I decided Danny must be a very good Christian at school as well as at church. He seemed to speak out boldly for Christ. I really liked that about him.

As a teenager, around 12 and up, I liked Danny, and he liked me. We weren't old enough to date, but we just said we liked each other. Then I decided I was tired of him, so I broke up with him. That happened about four times. After the fourth time, Danny decided he wasn't going to go with me anymore. So, when I decided I liked him again, he said he didn't like me. I asked him what was wrong, and he said he was tired of me breaking up with him. I told him I wouldn't do that again, but he decided to make me wait a while just to show me he wasn't going to jump whenever I wanted him to.

We were about 14 years old when this happened. So meanwhile, I decided to like other guys.

At this time, we were freshmen in high school. Danny decided he was going to date a girl from our church named Melissa, and I decided to date Allen, a guy who was asking me out at my high school. So, even though we both knew we were just waiting until Danny decided we would go together again, he dated Melissa and I dated Allen. Just so we both knew what we were doing and we hadn't changed our minds, we would wink at each other when we saw each other at church. That went on for

I wanted to serve God the best I knew how and raise a Christian family.

quite a long time. I knew Danny didn't really like Melissa because he told me he didn't, but I also knew he was pretty mad at me for breaking up with him so many times.

Going with a guy or breaking up was nothing to me. At that time, I didn't realize he was really crazy about me until his mother told my mother I had hurt him so badly he wouldn't eat and couldn't sleep. She told my mom he was very serious about me. She didn't know what to do with him. That was when I knew he liked me a lot. It was just a matter of waiting until he thought I had learned my lesson. So, I dated Allen for 2½ years while Danny and I kept winking at each other at church. He even bought me chocolates for Valentine's Day in secret. But no one knew what was going on. We did write letters sometimes—in code so no one would ever know what we said.

Finally, about midway through my junior year, Danny and I talked and decided to start going together again. We went out one evening and talked. He kissed me, and I remember thinking that I felt absolutely nothing. I wondered why and thought maybe I had no physical attraction for him, but I still wanted to go with him because he was a good Christian guy. Allen and I had no spiritual connection at all. We were so different we couldn't even talk about spiritual things. It was basically a closed subject. He did not understand my relationship with God nor my church and family. He was just a very nice guy, and I enjoyed his company.

Allen always treated me very well. He took me out to eat at nice places and took me to see symphony orchestras, plays, movies or just about anywhere I wanted to go. I knew he loved me and wanted to marry me because he kept mentioning it. Somehow I just never felt the kind of love I should feel for a husband, and I knew he and I would never marry. Meanwhile, he was a great guy to date and be friends with. I think Allen felt I would eventually change my mind, so he continued to treat me like a queen. Christmas time was like a shower for me. He bought me everything I could ever want. I felt bad about not having the money to do the same for him. Since he didn't work, I knew his parents were financing all of these gifts, meals, dates, etc. They really liked me, too. Somehow, I just couldn't make myself be in love with Allen. I knew it was a spiritual thing, and I couldn't overlook it.

Finally, I broke up with Allen, and Danny was going to break up with Melissa. However, that was not as easy as we thought it would be. By that time, Melissa had fallen head over heels in love with Danny, and Allen had fallen totally for me. In the process, Melissa almost had a nervous breakdown, and Allen refused to give up on us. I found Allen on a bridge watching Danny and me with binoculars one night. And Melissa came to me to talk about how heartbroken she was over Danny. It was a nightmare to say the least! My nerves got so bad, and I was trying to get through the rest of that school year! By the end of the year, Allen was graduating from high school and heading to Purdue University. My mother decided I needed to at least give Allen a present for graduation since he had always taken me out to nice restaurants, etc. She was right. Allen had spared no expense. He bought me everything he could think of and made me feel very special. So, I told Mom okay, we'd get him a gift for graduation. Mom took me to town, and we picked out a nice watch. I had no money, so of course, she paid for it, and we put it up at home for me to give him on graduation day.

Before graduation came, my mother invited Danny's parents over one evening. As they left, Mom showed them what I had purchased for Allen's graduation gift. Danny's parents were furious because I was supposed to be going with Danny, and they were determined I would not hurt him again. They went home and convinced him I was two-timing him. They basically refused to let him date me anymore.

After that, Danny did not talk to me for quite a while. He didn't take me out, nor did he tell me why. He was just very cold toward me. One night after church, I asked him if he could take me home from church. He agreed to take me—against his parents' advice. On the way, he asked me why I was seeing him and Allen at the same time. When I told him I wasn't, he told me the story about my mom showing his parents the watch I had gotten Allen for graduation. I was speechless! I told him the whole story, and we both realized my mother had planned this whole thing. My mother liked Allen and did not want me to go with Danny. What a dirty trick to play on us!

Later, my mom told me she was afraid I'd get serious about Danny, so she was trying to keep me away from him. Actually, I think that trick is what made me decide I *would* be serious about Danny. On that very night, Danny told me he was tired of all this breaking up and getting hurt. He said, "I will start dating you again under one condition. You have to promise you will never break up with me again." At that point, I was not really ready to be serious about anyone. However, because my mom had put me in this position, I felt I had to promise Danny I would never hurt him again that way. So, I promised. At that time, I was not fully aware of how painful it can be to be rejected. I was 17, and everything was a game to me. Even the idea of promising to never break up was not something I had really thought about ahead of time. I just thought I shouldn't hurt him again because he was serious about this. I knew he was a very good Christian, and I felt almost intimidated by his spirituality. I felt if he loved me that much, I was very lucky to find such a determined Christian guy.

After that, I just kept my word and never did break up with him again. When my friends at school asked me who I was going with, I would tell them he was a really good Christian guy from my church. I didn't think he was very cute, smart or attractive, so I wanted everyone to know he was a good Christian guy and that was enough for me. As time passed, I began to think he was attractive in his own way. His spirituality was what I really liked the most. Little by little, I was glad I chose to date him. I started loving him more each day.

Chapter 4

Change of Plans

Finally, in September of our first year of college, Dan (as he now wanted to be called) asked me to marry him. I told him I would, and we announced our engagement in the church bulletin and the local newspaper. He bought me a cedar chest as an engagement present. We set the date for early June 1966. I remember Dan telling me he was going to be a preacher and it was very important to him. He asked me if I would promise to back him and do my best to be a good preacher's wife. He told me all the cons about it so I would be aware of what I was getting into. I wasn't really excited about marrying a preacher, but I thought I would just have to learn to deal with it.

All this time, I never really thought ahead much or thought I wanted anything different. It was like this was my destiny, so I would go with the flow. It was like God had given me this opportunity to serve Him, so I would give it all I had. However, I had very strong doubts that I could ever make a good preacher's wife. Compared to the preachers' wives I had known, I was not like them at all. I just figured I'd have to be myself and let God use me the way He wanted to.

I was in Nursing School at a local hospital at that time. I was anxious to get away from home, and I'd be going to the same local junior college Dan was going to, so I decided to do it. I didn't really want to be a nurse, but I wanted to please my parents and my foster grandmother (the one who had taken my dad in to live with her and her brother). So, I went ahead and studied nursing. However, the blood and guts of nursing was not for me! I hated bed pans and sores. How I thought I could do all that was more than I can understand! I think I just jumped into it without thinking through what all it would entail. I made good grades and really enjoyed the book work, but as soon as they put me on the surgery floor in the hospital, I knew I had to get out of there. I could not change those surgical bandages and was afraid I'd be responsible for someone dying.

The talk of a wedding and realizing marriage was a serious commitment for life began to hit me. I became very serious about it and determined to be the best wife I could be. Plus, I knew I had found a good man. I also knew I had found a man who was the opposite personality of my father. I had always wished my dad could talk to me and show affection. I also wished he would compliment me and tell me he loved me—not scream at me and beat me when I made a mistake. Dan was a good communicator, and he made me feel loved. I really needed that. I loved my father, but I knew he wasn't able to be all I needed him to be as a father. So, I wanted to marry someone who would be able to do all the things my dad couldn't. I felt like Dan was that man.

As soon as we announced our wedding plans, my mother became very controlling. She came to the dorm sometimes just to talk to me. I think she was trying to stop me from seeing Dan so much. Even on Friday evenings, as I was ready to go out, she would come by and insist I go with her. It became very annoying. I knew what she was doing, but I felt like I couldn't tell her I had other plans. So I would go with her. It got pretty bad, and at one point, my parents tried to tell us not to get married. Dan got mad and slammed his fist on the cabinet and told them, "I'm going to marry your daughter whether you like it or not." It was pretty bad, and I was feeling very closed in as time went on. My mom went on making wedding plans with me, but told me she hadn't fully accepted our marriage. She said she was going to do all she could to convince me not to go through with it. It made things uncomfortable to say the least.

As things at home became very tense, I felt like I was being pulled apart. I made a very bad decision. Dan's parents were fighting and making him feel unloved. So, he turned to me for the love and attention he needed. In my mind, I thought, *"I'm going to be married in just a few months, so what's the big deal? I've been careful to keep myself for my husband and now I've found him. So, what could be wrong with having sex when you're engaged? I have never had sex with anyone else, so maybe this is okay." **(This decision was one of the worst I ever made in my*** *entire life!)* I felt a little guilty after the first time and told Dan I didn't think we should do this anymore until we were married. He didn't agree and convinced me it was okay.

A few weeks later, I found out I was pregnant. I was very nervous about telling my parents, but in a way I was glad. I was very anxious to get out of their house and be on my own. Plus, I knew they could not be against our marriage now. I had one problem that really surprised me—Dan acted like he had seen a ghost when I told him. He stammered around and acted like he didn't know what he was going to do. It was definitely not good news to him! I knew that but couldn't figure out why he was reacting like he did, so I just kind of ignored his response. After a few weeks, he told me his dad had told him he didn't have to marry me; he had a choice. I thought that was very cruel of his dad. Later, I wondered what Dan said to his dad to make him respond that way.

When I went to tell my parents I was pregnant, I was afraid they would disown me, so I wrote them a letter. To my surprise, my mother was very sympathetic. However, when she told her mother, my grandmother started having chest pains, and they were afraid she was having a heart attack. It turned out she was having an anxiety attack. I'm sure it was because she was remembering her own experience of being pregnant at 17 when she got married and all the problems involved. My grandmother confided in my mother and said, "I'm so afraid that Dan is just like her grandfather. I believe he has sexual problems, too, just like grandpa." My mother told me what she said later, but I thought Grandma was imagining things and silly for even thinking something like that.

By the time I was six weeks pregnant, Dan and I decided to elope. We thought we were going alone, but while I was getting ready to go, I noticed my mother and father getting all dressed up. I asked them where they were going. My mom said, "Well, you don't think you are getting married by yourself, do you?" I said, "Well, yes, I thought I was." She told me she and Dad were following us so they could be there when I got married. I hadn't really thought of it, but it was fine with me. Then I found out Dan's mom and dad were going, too. So, in all, there were nine people at our wedding, including the witnesses and preacher. We all drove to the next county for the wedding.

Dan ran late getting ready for our wedding. He said he'd been trying to find a pair of pajamas. Then, he cried all during our wedding! He cried a *lot!* At first, I thought he was just very happy, but later on, I began to really think about how he acted. I really believe he was crying because he ***had to get married!*** He never did get over that fact. It continued to bother him over the years! He went to counselor after counselor all the years of our marriage. He never felt like he had a choice. Even though our wedding was planned for just a few months later, Dan felt he had no choice in our getting married. I never could understand that. I thought of it as just getting married a few months early. Maybe it was the embarrassment because of his spiritual standing in the church. Maybe he somehow lost his identity at that point as a man of God. Maybe it was because he had been belittled as a boy for his natural male sexuality by his mother (as I found out later). I don't know. I do know he never got over it.

After our short wedding, Dan and I drove to Tennessee for the night. We came back home the next day. Our old car had a gas leak in the line, and I could smell gasoline coming back into the car as we drove. By the time we reached home, I was bleeding. I wasn't sure what this meant, but it continued for several days, and then I started having cramps. I told my mother, and she came over to see me. She advised me to get up and walk as much as I possibly could, which I did. It was very hard

She believed a lie from Satan, and it had ruined her life.

though. Finally, we called the doctor who had done my pregnancy test a few weeks earlier. He examined me and told me I was miscarrying. He wanted me to go to bed and said if I didn't stop bleeding soon, he'd have to put me in the hospital for a DNC. Of course, the bleeding and cramping only got worse. I finally gave in and went to the hospital for the surgery.

Afterwards, I was weak from losing so much blood but started feeling better right away. I was very troubled as to why my mother told me to walk as much as I could, and yet, the doctor put me to bed. Since I was only 17, I just did as they told me. I came to realize my mother was afraid I'd have a baby after being married only seven months, and the baby would be just like her—feeling unwanted and unloved. She thought it would be better for the baby to die than to go through what she'd gone through all her life. I so wished she could really know how much Grandma and Grandpa loved her. It was obvious to everyone—except her. She believed a lie from Satan, and it had ruined her life. If only she had quit listening to Satan's lies and hurtful thoughts!

After we were married, I dropped out of Nursing School and got a job at a factory close by. Dan worked part-time and completed his first year of junior college. By May, I had decided we needed to move to our church college that summer. Why wait a year? Dan needed to begin his Bible studies now. So I convinced him to think about moving. After a short period of time, he agreed. We began to make our plans to move. It was exciting, and I was looking forward to it very much.

Soon, we were all moved and settled in at college. I found a full-time job at the college registrar's office. That meant I could take courses free of charge. I enrolled for an evening class each semester just because I enjoyed learning. I especially enjoyed the Bible classes, Psychology and Sociology. I thought they were very interesting. Studying was more fun than work.

During those first years at church college, I was very happy. I enjoyed being with Christian people and taking the college classes very much. Dan was not quite so happy. He became very bitter over how the professors behaved. He thought their actions should match up to what our church teachings were, but they didn't always do that. Dan became more upset with the professors as time went on.

One day, I found a Playboy magazine under our front car seat. I asked Dan why it was there. He told me one of the guys must be pulling a joke on him, and he said he had not seen the magazine before. I thought maybe he was not telling the truth, but then maybe he had just been inquisitive. I had never seen a Playboy magazine myself. I was shocked at the pictures in it. Maybe Dan felt the same way. At least I was hoping that was the case. Up to that time, he had given me no reason to doubt him. He was very strict about his beliefs and very determined to follow God's calling on his life.

Chapter 5

Motherhood?

During our first four years of marriage, I had three miscarriages. Each time, the doctor said it was something different. The first miscarriage was just one month after we were married. I always thought it was from the gasoline leak in our old car.

When I was carrying our second baby, Dan decided he didn't want to attend our church college any longer. He thought they were all hypocrites, and he wanted to move home and get a secular job. He said he was through with all of this hypocrisy. Being a Christian was not what he had been taught it was. He was so disappointed with our church college. We moved back home so Dan could get a job. Just as we were moving home, I had a miscarriage and lost our second baby. This time, the doctor said it was from reaching too high. The cord had wrapped around the baby's neck and shut off the air.

After we moved back home, got an apartment and Dan had a full-time job, I became pregnant with our third baby. I started having trouble in my third month. It was a very difficult pregnancy. I was put on bed rest or at least no working or moving around much. My parents moved a mobile home onto their three-acre country lawn, and I enjoyed the country air and tranquility while I tried to finish out my pregnancy. But my kidneys were unable to void all of the poison from my body as well as the baby's. I suffered from toxemia and very high blood pressure from three months along until our third baby was stillborn at 7½ months.

The days there in the country before the miscarriage had been so sweet! God's Presence was so near to me as I sat in the yard reading my Bible and praying. I felt as if God Himself came down and sat with me. I felt such peace and complete joy! Later, I wondered if God was preparing me for what was to come. I know during those months of waiting, I became so close to God that I leaned on Him totally. I trusted Him completely. I knew He loved me, and I wanted to be as close to Him as I possibly could. Some days, I wouldn't have cared if God took me home with Him, right then. I was ready to spend eternity by His side. Earthly things took on a whole new perspective when I was in God's Presence.

During this time of our marriage, Dan was working on plans for opening a nightclub with a friend of his. He was far from where God wanted him to be. He had become someone I didn't really like. He wasn't easy to live with, and I guess I was glad he wasn't home a lot. I was supposed to stay calm, and he didn't seem to care. It didn't seem to be important to him that my blood pressure was at stroke stage. I had a friend of mine, Anita, stay with me through those very tough months. She made sure I was resting and eating and doing okay physically. The doctor told us I needed someone with me 24/7 until I went into labor. Anita was the perfect caretaker.

When I was seven months pregnant, the doctor told me to have my bag ready the next week when I came in for my appointment. He was sending me to the hospital to take the baby. He felt the baby was far enough along to make it, and I needed to be free from the pressure the baby was putting on my kidneys. Of course, I was excited and began looking forward to the big day. We prepared the nursery, and I thought the waiting was over. That weekend, I had a terrible spell with my blood pressure. I became very weak, saw stars and had to lie down for quite some time in order to get my sight back completely. After that, I started feeling better and went on getting ready for my doctor's appointment on Tuesday. I did notice after the spell on Sunday afternoon, I didn't feel the baby kicking anymore. I was concerned but kept telling myself it was okay. I was feeling much better so everything was going to be fine.

My trip to the doctor on Tuesday was not at all what I expected. The doctor took forever to read my chart after examining me. He turned the pages over and over and over. I thought, *"What in the world is he doing? Why is he not saying anything?"* Finally, he turned around and said, "I'm sorry, your pregnancy has terminated." My mind would not accept what he was saying so I thought, *"Of course my pregnancy has terminated. I'm going to the hospital to have the baby. I knew that."* I didn't say a word as he stood there looking at the floor. The doctor again looked at me and said, "Do you understand what I just said?" I shook my head slowly as if to say I did. About that time, I noticed my mother was sitting there bawling. The doctor looked at me again and gently said, "Your baby is dead." Wow! I couldn't twist that around no matter how hard my mind tried. The doctor looked at my mother and told her he'd be back shortly. She nodded, and he left the room.

It took just a few seconds for me to start processing what he had said. *The baby had died? How could that be? I had done everything they told me to do. I ate right. I rested. What could have gone wrong?* As I sat there thinking, I recalled the doctor previously telling me this had to be my last pregnancy. My kidneys were failing, and I could never live through another pregnancy. If this pregnancy terminated, I would never be able to get pregnant again. Wow, this was devastating! About that time, a nurse walked into my room. She came over to me and said, "Honey, don't give up. I had seven miscarriages before I finally had my daughter. Just never give up." For some reason, that nurse seemed to be the one voice I paid attention to that day. It was as if God was saying to me, *"It's just not the right timing. Do not worry; you'll be a mother one day."* After that, I grieved very deeply for my baby, but I never gave up on having my own children one day. I never told anyone how I felt. I knew my parents and Dan would try to convince me otherwise. They were so afraid I would die if I ever tried to have another baby. My kidneys showed severe damage from carrying this baby for 7½ months—too much damage to ever make it through another pregnancy. The doctor said we would make plans to tie my tubes shortly after my body was recovered from the trauma it had been through. He advised me to wait a couple of years before having the surgery.

Then he sent me home to carry the baby until I went into labor naturally. He said it could be up to two weeks, and my body needed the extra time to heal since it had been under such a strain. Waiting would give the poison from my kidneys time to drain out, and my blood pressure would get back to normal. He told me he had been very concerned about which of us would survive or if we could both make it through this to delivery. He said he was glad I was alive and he wouldn't have wanted to deliver a baby without a mother to take care of her. Nothing he said alleviated my shock or my pain from knowing my baby had died. It was all just chatter, and it didn't help me at all. Nor did the idea of walking around with a baby inside me I knew was dead, seem real to me. So what do I say to everybody when they say, "How far along are you?" or "What are you having?" I was petrified at the idea of having to wait two weeks before delivering the baby. I decided I would not go anywhere. I would just stay home and rest. I couldn't handle telling people what was happening, and I knew they would be asking—they always do.

After that, I had several nights of nightmares, and I started trying to stay awake, just so I could have peace of mind. My mind was so grieved over my baby's death, I couldn't think of anything else. Everything reminded me I was pregnant with a dead baby. I also had visions of what she probably looked like by now, after dying. It was a terrible experience!

Finally, God gave me a vision (a very real, live vision) of my little girl standing at *Heaven's Gate*, waiting for me. She was beautiful and happy in a frilly pink dress, with curly, light brown hair and flowers in her hand. It was as if she was anxiously waiting for me to come with her to Heaven. I never grieved over her in nightmares again. Thank God for that vision! The nightmares were gone forever. Sure, I grieved that I didn't have her. I still miss her even many years later, but she was so happy and beautiful in Heaven with my Savior. How could I ask her to come back? The vision changed my grieving completely. It was okay. Even though I missed her terribly, I knew she was okay now. I look forward to the day we'll be together, where there will be no more tears and no more parting, in God's eternity.

It was four days before I went into labor. I had labor pains all night long but thought I would wait until everyone else had a good night's sleep and then we would head to the hospital the next morning. At 7:00 a.m., I woke everybody up and told them I needed to head to the hospital. My husband and mother did not believe me when I said I needed to hurry. The doctor had told us I could not deliver this baby on my own because the baby would not be giving me any help. He recommended taking my time when coming to the hospital so I wouldn't have to lie there looking at four walls waiting for delivery.

I insisted we go now, so my mother decided to check and see if I was actually ready to deliver. All at once, her face turned white, and she became extremely nervous, which was very odd for her; she was always so in control! I knew then I was in trouble. She said, "The baby has a full head of hair, I saw it." She grabbed several layers of clothing and wrapped them around me, and she told Dan to pull the car as close as possible to the house as quickly as he could.

We hurried to the hospital which was about twenty miles away. I lay in the back seat while Dan drove, and my mother sat in the front with him. Both of them were quite nervous. On the way to the hospital, my labor pains stopped. As we arrived at the hospital ER entrance, my mother jumped out of the car and immediately had everyone moving at top speed. All I knew or even cared about was that I was finally going to have this baby. Everything was a blur—people talking, whispering, doctors, nurses—everything. I knew at one point my fingernails were turning blue and the nurse was worried. Then my doctor asked me to not look at the baby. He said she was deformed from all the poison in my body. His face turned very white, and he looked sick as he delivered the baby. The anesthesiologist arrived just as they were wheeling me out of the delivery room. I went through the whole delivery with no anesthetic. I was just glad to have it over.

The doctor kept me in the hospital for a few days while I recuperated. I could not even be released in time for the baby's funeral. My mother and Dan had to pick out my little girl's dress and casket as well as make funeral arrangements. They brought pictures of the dress to the hospital to show me. A friend of mine, Jenny, stayed with me at the hospital during the funeral. I will never forget looking up at Jenny's face that day. Big tears were streaming down her cheeks as she just sat by my side. I remembered she had also had a miscarriage not long before that day. Without her saying a word, I knew she felt my pain. Somehow that released my emotions that had been penned up inside me, and I began to cry, too. It was such a healing time for me to just sit and cry with my friend. God knew what I needed that day, and He sent the perfect person to help me get through this time of deep pain. God always knows exactly what I need and provides it so well.

After the funeral, guilt began to eat Dan up. Because of the baby's death, he felt God was punishing him *(which I don't believe was true)*. So, he decided to go back to college and preach as he knew God had called him to do. I was so glad to hear *that* news! I knew Dan was miserable pretending to be this big sinner who wanted nothing to do with God. It was not him at all. He was just responding from the disappointment he had from watching people and taking his eyes off of the only perfect person who ever lived—Jesus.

Once I was released from the hospital, my friend, Anita, and I decided we needed to go out and apply for jobs. I was actually doing very well physically and needed to keep busy now. We walked all over the downtown part of the nearby city trying to decide where we wanted to apply. I had always wanted to be a telephone operator; I thought it would be lots of fun. So I went in and put my application in at AT&T®. Anita said I was wasting my time. They had been on strike and wouldn't be hiring any time soon. I decided I wanted to have my application in there just in case they needed someone.

To my surprise, about two days later, I received a call to come in to AT&T to take a test. They were ending their strike and were planning to hire soon. I took the test, passed it and was hired to start working as a long distance operator right away. I loved my job. I couldn't wait to get to work each day. It was interesting, challenging, and the days just flew by. I was having so much fun! It wasn't like work at all. The pay was very good, too, plus the benefits were excellent. I felt so excited that God had given me the perfect job to keep my mind occupied all day while I adjusted to the death of my baby. It was just perfect!

I felt a special nudge one night to call Anita from work. I told her to get up to AT&T and get her application in. They were hiring 14 new people. She could be one of them. Anita applied right away and was hired a few weeks later. She was placed in Directory Assistance. Since she worked across the hall from me, I didn't get to see her very much. Anita continued to work at AT&T until she retired. God knew then how much she would need to have a good job. She had many hard years ahead of her when her husband came home from the war in Vietnam. His body and nervous system were severely affected by the war. She told me he was never the same after the war, which is so typical of many of our men who fight for our country and freedom. The operator job also helped me to put Dan through college. It even allowed me to take college courses which my company paid for. Sometimes, we just have to listen to that small little voice or that nudge saying, *"Go on in there and apply"* or *"Make that phone call."* That company was a blessing to Dan and I for years to come as it was to Anita.

It wasn't until probably a year later, when we were back in college, that I was standing in church one Sunday evening as the pastor was calling for anyone who needed prayer to come forward. I felt a definite nudge to go forward and ask God to heal me so I could have children. I walked to the front of our church of about 400 people. I knelt at the altar and our pastor's wife came over to pray with me. She asked me what I wanted to pray about, and I told her I had been told I would never have children, but I wanted God to heal me and give me a family. We prayed a simple prayer for my healing, and I went back to my seat. A burden lifted, and I knew I had been obedient to what God had asked me to do. I never discussed it with anyone—only God, my pastor's wife and I knew what took place that day. The two of us agreed in prayer, and I knew God heard us.

In the fall of 1969, my doctor decided I needed to have my tonsils removed. They were continually infected, and he was afraid they would cause too much poison in my system. I scheduled the surgery and had my tonsils pulled with no problems whatsoever. After surgery, before I was released to go home, my doctor came in and told me he had taken x-rays of my kidneys just to see if there had been any changes since last year. Totally shocked, he explained he had called five other specialists in to confirm what he thought he saw. All five specialists were in complete agreement. "The kidneys you have now are not the same kidneys you had a year ago! There was no way of comparing the old and new x-ray pictures." They all said I had brand new kidneys! No one had an explanation, only that the kidneys I had now were perfect—no damage or sign of any damage! The doctor was puzzled but tried to say maybe somehow my kidneys had matured or something. It was a real puzzle to all of the doctors called in. Other organs might heal and repair, but kidneys do *not* repair themselves. I knew exactly what had happened, but I just let them all try to figure it out. I figured no one would listen to me anyway. I was only 21 years old, and they obviously didn't know God could heal. They never once gave Him any credit at all. I just kept all of these things in my heart and thanked God for hearing my prayer and healing my body.

The doctor recommended I wait until springtime to try to get pregnant, just in case my kidneys weren't as strong as they looked. That would give me the summer months to get a good start on the pregnancy before I might catch a winter cold. Then they would constantly watch me the whole time just to be sure nothing went wrong. He was still very much afraid, but decided it looked like I would be okay to have a baby now. He was quite right. I was very much okay. I never had kidney problems again—*ever* in my whole life! I am writing this story, 46 years later, and to this day, I have strong healthy kidneys. When God does something, He does it right! I have no doubt He's the only one who can heal kidneys, and He answered my prayer. No one else but one person even knew what I prayed.

The next June, I became pregnant again. This time, it was a great pregnancy. Everything went well until the end. The doctor told me the baby would be born breach, bottom first. That could be a problem. So they would not let me go more than 15 hours in hard labor. They said they would take the baby if I struggled more than 15 hours. My grandmother came to stay with me for the last six weeks of my pregnancy. She and I had wonderful times together, talking about the Lord and painting crafts, reading and praying. It was such a great six weeks! I actually hated that the time had to end, but finally the day came.

My water broke at 6:00 a.m., and we headed to the hospital. At 9:30 p.m. that night, I delivered my very first live baby! Daniel weighed 8 lbs. 7 oz. It was an extremely hard delivery. I even started bleeding through the pores of my skin toward the end. At that point, the doctor asked me to push hard, and he pulled the baby out, and it was over. What a day! I was so excited, yet so exhausted. I could barely stay awake to let people know I was okay. Then I slept for several hours. It wasn't until the next morning, when I looked in the mirror, that I saw blood all over my face and shoulders. That's when they told me they had thought they might lose me. And why they told me to push one last time as they pulled the baby out. I was just glad it was all over, and the baby was healthy and doing well. He was black and blue all over, so the nurses called him "The Bruiser." He looked like he'd been in a fight, and he was big enough too! They put him under a light because he had jaundice. The light helped his cuts and bruises too. Everybody who came by wondered why that big baby was under the light. He was too big to be a preemie. And why was he all beat up? He was the talk of the nursery.

Our pastor came up to see me and my baby. I did my best to talk him out of going to the nursery. I apologized over and over for the way Daniel looked. Soon, however, Daniel was healed, and his skin was beautiful from being under the lights for so long. Even though he did have to stay in the hospital for two weeks after he was born, I was just glad he was alive and coming home. One day, as I was holding him, I remember just crying and crying. I thanked God for a baby with ten fingers and ten toes. A healthy body and all I could ever wish for was now here in reality. It was almost more than I could take in. I was so thankful. It was my "dream come true!" God gave me the desire of my heart, and I would do my best to raise him as God instructed me, for he truly was a gift from God.

*When God does
something, He
does it right!*

Chapter 6

I'm a Freak!

Dan began to have a lot of problems and went to many, many counselors and psychologists. Every psychologist and counselor told him (and me) the same thing—that he had a "mother problem" not a marriage problem. They said he felt his mother had belittled him so much about manhood that he had a very low self-esteem problem. One counselor told me Dan allowed him to hypnotize him. While hypnotized, he was asked to stand in front of a mirror and describe himself. He described himself as if he were a freak! While describing himself, the counselor said Dan cried the biggest tears he had ever seen. It was so bad the counselor told me to never allow him to handle the checkbook, money or any other important paperwork in our house. He said, "Dan has such a bad opinion of himself he will sabotage anything he does right before he is successful. He doesn't believe he deserves to receive any type of success, so he will always do something to make himself fail." I felt so sorry for him. I knew his mother loved him dearly, and he was surely mistaken about how she felt about him, but it didn't matter. He was convinced he was worthless and deserved only failure.

During one counseling session, Dan decided he needed time to figure out if he wanted to remain married or not. His counselor asked me to come to the office, and we discussed me going to stay at my parents' home for a while. He told me Dan needed time to think about what he really wanted in life. The counselor felt it would be best if I was gone until he could decide for himself if he really wanted this marriage and family. He advised me not to push him in any way. Just leave him alone until he made a decision and called to tell me the answer. I was quite disturbed but decided to do as the counselor advised. In my heart, I felt sure Dan would want us back, so I just prayed and left him alone. It was about two weeks before I heard from him about his decision. He said he definitely wanted us back into his life. He asked us to come home right away. So we did.

I began to be more convinced of what the counselor told me about Dan's destructive behavior as I started to observe his actions. If he had the checkbook, he would overdraw and cost us tons of money in overdraft charges. I tried to handle the finances myself to avoid this, but it was hard because he was determined to write bad checks. He appeared to be very selfish, but I don't know, maybe he was just sabotaging our finances as the counselor said. The one time he showed that he refused to be successful the most was the semester before his graduation from college. He decided to leave college and accept an associate pastor's position during his last semester in college. He did not have a heavy load academically. He just wanted to drop out of college right before he graduated.

That same year, Dan also used bad judgment as a senior high youth leader at our local church. He would often take a particular high school girl home from youth activities alone, with no one else in the car—just him and her. As they were decorating the church basement for a Halloween Party, the girl kissed him. Others were present, and it got back to the main youth pastor. Dan was called into the church office to explain himself. He acted like he didn't understand why it happened, so he was moved out of the senior high group and placed in college age student leadership. I was not told what happened, but I knew something wasn't right. Everyone seemed to know what was going on except me. No one said a word to me. All I knew was what Dan told me, which was that he was moved to the college students' class, and he didn't want to move. I thought he was being edged out of the senior high youth by a guy Dan had asked to help us. I felt sorry for him but knew how politics can work sometimes.

"Dan has such a bad opinion of himself he will sabotage anything he does right before he is successful."

It wasn't until three years later Dan told me he had feelings for the high school girl, and she had kissed him in the church basement. At that time, it seemed a little mysterious to me that he hadn't told me earlier. It made me think he was very guilty, but at that time, I didn't feel like I needed to break up a marriage over a three-year-old mistake. It did cause me to wonder what was wrong though when he made the statement that the 16-year-old girl was very attractive to him because she reminded him of me at that age. I was still in my early twenties and weighed the same as I did at age 16. How could I look that much different than I had eight or nine years ago? I really didn't! It all still remained somewhat of a mystery, but I just dismissed it and went on.

Right after this incident happened, Dan left me a note that he was headed to the nearby river with his gun. He was tired of living and just wanted to end it all. Of course it scared me, and I called our youth pastor. He had me come to the house, and he told me he was so sorry they had dismissed Dan from the senior high group. He said, "I just knew that wasn't right." After several hours, Dan came home saying he couldn't go through with it. The youth pastor still felt terrible about all of this. I felt he did everything he could to help Dan rise above everything that happened. In fact, I believe it was our youth pastor who recommended Dan for an associate pastor's position soon after this incident.

Right at the beginning of Dan's last semester of college, he received an invitation to relocate, to be an associate pastor, day care director and music director for a church. Rather than wait, he wanted to move as soon as possible. Instead of finishing his last semester of college, he dropped out and accepted the position right then. It never did make a lot of sense to me. I just went along with it for the sake of avoiding confrontation. He wasn't in the best of spirits. I thought maybe it would help him come out of the depression he had been in. After all, my thinking was that he had been accused of doing something wrong, and he was completely innocent! I decided he was having trouble facing those who were lying about him, and he wanted to get away. I figured he would get his degree later. So, off we went.

Chapter 7

Is This Candid Camera?

Dan did very well as the music director and day care director in the new church. Everyone was very pleased with his work, and the senior pastor even let him preach occasionally. So he began to preach, and he seemed to really enjoy that part of his job. The one drawback of this assignment was the pastor's wife. She would sit in church and wink at Dan as he sat on the platform. When I went with her on a youth trip, she flirted with the teen director's husband right in front of me. She rubbed his leg as he drove the RV, and she made eyes at him and openly rubbed on him in a very sexual way. She watched me to see what my response would be and basically flaunted herself over and over with this man in my presence. She had just gone through a hysterectomy and was going through serious hormonal problems or an early menopause. She was having a very hard time, and I truly felt sorry for her husband. He was a good man and was trying very hard to keep her happy, as well as run the church. It just wasn't working. I could see why he needed an assistant. I doubt very seriously he knew just how badly his wife was acting. If he did know, he never let on to anyone.

One day, she told me she would give me advice on how to keep my man, if I wanted it. From the very sexual way she said it, I knew she was in big trouble. I never took her up on her offer because I could feel the evil in her eyes when I was with her and couldn't trust her at all.

Dan told me he couldn't go inside the parsonage when her husband was gone because he was afraid she would attack him. He said she always flirted with him and said very sexually enticing things to him when he came to the door. It was a terrible situation to be in. I always believed him concerning her for some reason—maybe because I wanted to or maybe because she was in her forties and had just had a hysterectomy. I guess I thought she was too old for him. We were only 24 and 25 at that time.

It was our first full-time church position. Wow! Did we ever get broken in right from the beginning! I became very much aware of how Satan attacks preachers and their families. It was an eye-opening experience for me. I could see we had a wonderful pastor, but Satan was doing his best to destroy him through his wife's sickness. We only stayed in that church for 14 months. We were very anxious to move on. So when we received a call from another church in the area, in the spring of 1973, we jumped at the chance to move.

The new church was a small church where the senior pastor, Pastor Stephen, had convinced the church board to hire Dan as the music director and associate pastor for $30 a week salary. This meant Dan had to work outside the church, and so did I. I went back to work at AT&T to make a living for us, and Dan worked at a factory. This left us little time to be at home together. While we were in this location, Dan's sister, Sandra, also came to live with us. We had been friends with Pastor Stephen's family in college. Their two boys had been in our youth group. Sandra started dating their middle son, Bill, while we were working there in the church.

I began taking organ lessons and found out I *loved* playing the organ! After a little encouragement, I became the church organist and loved playing for each service. It just felt like I was doing what I was supposed to do. The organ had been sitting untouched for quite some time. The congregation was happy to have someone playing it. I really enjoyed every minute of playing it, especially to praise and worship my heavenly Father. He had blessed me so much. I wanted to praise Him all I could. The organ seemed to be my special way of doing just that.

While we were there, Dan and I formed a quartet with another couple. We sang for a revival service and whenever we were needed. That was a lot of fun for me. I loved it. The people in the church were very good people, although they were pretty legalistic, but I think that came from Pastor Stephen and his wife Lenore. It was never a problem for me. I was always pretty conservative anyway. I think Sandra had more problems with the legalism than I did. I remember her wishing Lenore wasn't so legalistic, but she got along with her anyway. I really believe Pastor Stephen's true desire to be close to God caused

Dan to live as close to God as he could. He was very outspoken, and he kept Dan accountable. It was a very good two years for our family.

Our second child, Mark, was born during that time, and the church made it a good experience for us. In my third or fourth month of the pregnancy, my doctor could not find a heartbeat and sent me to the hospital for a sonogram (which was only done in emergencies at that time). It really scared me! I told our pastor's wife, Lenore, because I was so upset. I will never forget her response. She said, "Well, you didn't really want this baby anyway, did you?" I remember being really shocked. *Of course I want this baby! Why would she even think I didn't? If she only knew how badly I want to have children and that I have already lost three babies, she would know I am thrilled to be having another baby!* Lenore was just being herself, so I dismissed it and never did tell her how shocked I was at her question.

That incident, however, stuck in my head from then on. What a crazy thing to say to a woman who is worried about losing a baby! Even if a pregnancy isn't planned, losing a baby is a very hard thing to deal with emotionally. Saying you didn't want it anyway would make it all that much harder to handle. Lenore was never a very tactful person, but that was probably the worst I had heard from her. It did teach me a lesson though. Never say things like that to a woman who is losing a baby. It could devastate her! I put that in my memory bank, just in case I needed it someday.

Of course, the sonogram showed Mark was alive and well. I had a young doctor, the only gynecologist in town, so I assumed he just panicked because he didn't hear the heartbeat and didn't realize how scared I would become. I didn't have any more trouble during my pregnancy with Mark. Things went quite well from that point on. I worked the first few months and then stayed home when I got toward the end of the pregnancy. My grandmother came to stay with me the last six weeks of the pregnancy, just as she had when Daniel was on the way. We had a good time talking and playing with Daniel who was three at that time. Grandma was such a help. She made my waiting time much more pleasant. We talked about spiritual things and the Bible. She gave me such wonderful advice I will never forget. Her love for God was always written all over her face; she could never hide it. It was that love that had made me long for the same kind of relationship with God, and it became my lifelong goal to have it!

A really crazy thing happened to me while we were serving there! I couldn't move my legs very well the last six weeks of my pregnancy. Because of that, I didn't play the organ for six weeks. Of course, no one else knew how to play the organ, so it was not played during that time. Pastor Stephen never could understand why I couldn't continue playing. He was quite put out with my decision not to play for six weeks. I never did address his question as to why I couldn't play it. I thought it would be evident to anyone who really thought about it. It is very difficult to move both feet and both hands while trying to balance yourself on an organ bench when you are eight or nine months pregnant. Isn't that obvious to anyone? Plus, climbing up onto the bench was an ordeal, too. It was high off the floor and up in front of the entire congregation. It seemed almost immodest for me to even try to get up on that bench, to say nothing of how hard it was to move my feet and legs once I got up there. It was just too much for me at that point. I felt embarrassed even trying to explain to the pastor why I couldn't do it. So, I just laughed to myself and went on my way.

When my delivery day came, we called my mom, and she came to town and waited with us. It was very exciting to share everything with both my mother and my grandmother. They were a sense of security to me. I loved having them there. It was especially nice to have them there during this particular wait. I got up on the day I was scheduled to go to the hospital to be induced. The baby hadn't come before the due date, so the doctor told me to come to the hospital at 6:00 a.m. on July 16. He wanted to induce my labor. After a sleepless night, I got up at 5:00 a.m. and headed to the hospital. I arrived at the hospital, bag in hand, ready to finally have this baby. As we walked up to the check-in desk, I gave my name to the receptionist. To my surprise, she said, "If you aren't having hard labor pains, would you go home and come back tomorrow morning?" My mouth fell open, and I just stared at her in unbelief. I turned and looked at Dan. Finally I said, "Is this Candid Camera?" Dan assured me it was not. Then, the truth of the situation began to dawn on me. I was going to have to turn around, go back home and wait another day before I could get a bed in this hospital. As unbelievable as that seemed, it was true. So that's what we did. I was so glad I had my mother and grandmother at home to help me get through that last day. I needed all the encouragement I could get. The disappointment of having to come back home was almost more than I could handle.

Then, on July 17, I got up again at 5:00 a.m., went to the hospital and checked in at the receptionist desk again. This time she had a bed, and I was allowed to be admitted. I was finally, truly going to have this baby! Mark weighed only 6 lbs. 12 oz., and I was so glad. The small town hospital and doctors were not what I'd been used to. My doctor didn't even make it to the hospital to deliver Mark. His dad, an older general practitioner, came in the delivery room. He didn't believe in anything except a local anesthetic, so that's all I got. I was just happy the labor only lasted a couple of hours, and the delivery was quick. Even then, my mother ended up coming to the labor room, calling a nurse for me and telling them I was having the baby. They were just leaving me in my

God knew ahead of time, and His timing is always so perfect.

room to suffer, with no one checking me. It was as if I was just visiting the hospital. No one seemed to understand I was having a baby and needed help. Of course, when my mother took over, things changed. The nurses asked me to hold off and stop pushing. Then they had to get a chair for Dan to sit in because he was passing out. Finally, I delivered Mark. He was red-headed and light skinned. He looked nothing like Daniel. I was so glad it was all over, and we were both well. God knew where to put me when I had trouble and where to put me when everything needed to go smoothly. I don't know what I would have done there in that country hospital if I had any problems. I don't feel like they were equipped to handle anything out of the ordinary. God knew ahead of time, and His timing is always so perfect.

Mark was allergic to everything! What a time we had! He slept days and woke up at night. After I took him home, he had terrible colic, and I was so tired. I just couldn't seem to get any sleep. Daniel got up at 5:00 a.m., right after

Mark went to sleep. I thought I'd never catch up on sleep. Going back to work didn't help. That meant I was tired all the time and had less opportunity to rest. Soon, I started having terrible headaches and nothing seemed to help them.

The headaches got worse and worse until they were lasting all day and all night. I couldn't get rid of them. I was sent to a specialist who found I had had brain damage for quite some time at the base of my brain, in the back. It had become inflamed and was causing me to have constant pain. (I had trouble with severe headaches all my life, even as a preschooler, but the doctors could never figure out why.) The doctor put me on a medicine for the inflammation and soon my pain was gone. He told me to stay on the medicine because my brain damage caused a weak spot in my brain. He said that any time I became tired or sick, the damaged spot would be the most likely place for inflammation to flare up. I began taking the medication daily. It was such a blessing to be rid of the headaches! I was able to work now and enjoy life so much more. It was a different world!

Working at AT&T wasn't always easy for me. I was always afraid Dan wasn't watching the kids very well. He was so easily entranced by the TV. I remember having to call him on the phone during the evening just so he would have to be distracted from the TV and check on the babies. Then I'd call on my break just to be sure he was alert to what they were doing. I always asked him if they had eaten or what they'd been doing so he would have to think about it. I had to trust God to take care of them because I knew Dan didn't always pay attention to what they were doing, and I knew they were too little to be left with him, but I felt I had no choice. He wanted to watch the boys in the evenings while I worked so we didn't have to pay a babysitter. I was nervous about it but just did my best. I felt God knew my situation and would keep them safe. I had to miss quite a few church services also while I worked, but I couldn't choose my hours, so I just worked and did my best.

After serving two good years there, we got a call from my uncle who was pastoring at a church down south. He wanted us to come visit him. My uncle felt like we would do very well pastoring a small church in that area. He had recommended us to his area oversight and wanted us to interview with him.

Dan decided to take him up on his offer, so we made plans to visit my uncle and aunt. After we interviewed with the area supervisor, we both knew we'd be moving south very soon. Pastor Stephen wanted us to stay in the area where we were, as did many other people. We interviewed for a church close by, but neither of us felt it was the right move, so we turned it down.

Chapter 8

Did You Just Call Me a "Coon Ass"?

The new church was very small, but we both felt it was where God wanted us. It was also 1,000 miles south, but we knew it was right. God must have had a reason for sending us there. He impressed on us very strongly this was the place we needed to be.

It was April, 1975, when we moved south. While Dan drove the big moving truck, I drove our van with Daniel (4) and Mark (9 months). Sandra helped me some but kept falling asleep. It was a horrific move for me. I was sick the whole time. As we were driving there, I kept pulling over to throw up, and I was so nauseated; it made the trip miserable. I thought I'd never get to our destination! I began to wonder if I could be pregnant. After being bawled out for stopping so many times and running to the bathroom, I finally told Dan. I don't know if he believed me or not, but I thought maybe he would stop telling me I couldn't stop to go to the bathroom if he knew I was actually vomiting and not just going to the bathroom.

Our new assignment was in Southern Louisiana. It was a very odd-looking little town to me. Coming from Northern Illinois, it was definitely a culture shock. It looked like a ghost town to me. I was shocked to find business was actually being conducted in the town's stores each week. They looked like the store fronts in the old western movies I'd seen on TV. It was hard to believe they were for real.

The mixture of the Southern/Cajun language was very hard to get used to. I found myself saying, "Pardon me," continually. I especially remember someone continually saying the word "Coon Ass" to me. I thought they were cussing at me for some reason, but I had no idea why. Later, I found out everyone from Louisiana was called "Coon Ass," and they were proud of it. Even their Governor said it on TV.

When we moved to Louisiana, I was supposed to be able to transfer within AT&T. However, when I went to AT&T for my physical, before I began work, I found out I *was* pregnant again. AT&T informed me they had a policy not to train anyone during a pregnancy. Therefore, I could not work until after the baby was born. What a disappointment that was!

The snakes, bugs, alligators, Spanish moss and swamps were all so foreign to me. It was as if I was in another country. And the food was so spicy hot, I couldn't even eat it. The daytime heat made me so sick I had to stay indoors from 10:00 a.m. to sundown so I wouldn't pass out—per the doctor's instructions. I have never gone through such a traumatic time of adjustment! Being pregnant made it so much harder. My hormones were going crazy! I cried for the first year we were there. One good thing about living there was the humidity. Because of the humidity, Mark's congestion and sinus problem cleared up immediately, and he became very healthy. No more congestion and colds and his allergies all seemed to go away. He thrived in the Louisiana weather!

Our new little church consisted of three women and their children (14 total)! I became the church pianist and/or organist and teen Sunday school teacher. I also wrote an article for the local newspaper each week about our church news. The church had one solid, reliable member, Mrs. Williams, who was 62 years old. Mrs. Williams became my best friend. I don't know what I would have done without her. She and her husband owned the town grocery store. It was a part of the town's storefronts that looked so ancient to me. The nearest supermarket was about fifteen to twenty miles away. Williams Grocery had very high prices, and since we only made $30 a week plus housing, I couldn't afford to buy my groceries there. I drove to a larger city every other week to get our groceries.

Our new little town had very little opportunity for employment, and we couldn't live on $30 a week. Right away, the church gave us a raise to $40 a week, but even then we needed more income. Dan decided to work in the woods as a logger. It was tough work, but he did it for several months until he finally got a job at a gas station close to home. That was such a blessing for him to be able to work better hours and not do such hard, physical work.

The church started growing right away. First, we decided to clean out the sanctuary. There was actually a pile of lumber on one side of the sanctuary. We got the lumber out and used it to fix up the church. We painted the building and fixed it up as best we could. We even poured a slab of cement in front of the church to make a sidewalk. The church sat on stilts and in front of the church was a big mud puddle. Pouring the cement was a step of faith. It cost $50, which we didn't have, but we knew the church needed that sidewalk. We prayed and then we poured the cement one afternoon and received a donation that very evening of $50 from someone who didn't even attend our church. God rewarded us for stepping out in faith. Soon the attendance was running in the 40's, and we actually had some men start coming to church. Our one stable member, Mrs. Williams, saw her 39-year-old son and his family saved, and he was called to preach. During the two years we pastored this church, four young men came to God who later answered their call to preach. Even though it was a tough experience, it was well worth everything we went through.

One incident took place only three weeks after we arrived in the little town that was very nerve-wracking. Once I really thought about it, I realized how God protected us and how He had His hand on us and that church during the entire time we served there. The mother of a young man who also helped play piano for the church called me on a Wednesday night, right before the service. She had not attended church that I could remember, and I had trouble understanding her accent. I did know she was extremely upset with me, and it seemed she was ready to come to the service and set everyone straight. Just as I was ready to go to church, I noticed one of my children had a fever, so I decided not to take them out that night. I did feel I should warn Dan she had called and was very upset. Everything else that happened was told to me by church members and Dan.

During the service, the lady came in and sat right up front. She carried with her a terribly hateful spirit. Though Dan didn't know her very well, she seemed to want to pick an argument with him—right in the middle of the service. They had testimonies from the congregation, and the lady decided she needed to say something. She gave a kind of "you're no better than me" testimony. It was obvious to everyone there that night she was trying to cause problems. There was a lot of tension around her, and it was distracting to everyone in the service. As everyone was praying, Dan prayed God would deliver us from any demonic spirit that would try to destroy our church. He bound the demon and prayed it would never be allowed to work in our church again. Some people in the congregation were aware of why he prayed that way and agreed with him in prayer. Others seemed oblivious to his prayer. From that moment on, the troubled lady kept her mouth shut. She sat through the church service, then left as soon as it was over.

The next day, we received a phone call from the lady's family saying she left our service, got in her car and drove straight across the border to a neighboring state without telling anyone. She was killed in a head-on collision there. No one in her family even knew why she had taken off like that or why she had gone in that direction. The whole family was very bewildered when they got the call from an out-of-state Police Department to come identify their wife and mother. Only the people from our congregation who were present that night in the prayer meeting knew what had happened, and they were all in shock.

Dan was asked to preach the funeral. As you can imagine, it was an extremely hard service to preach. This was our first senior pastorate, and our first month was unbelievable for us all. I will never forget the feeling of shock *and* awe we had over this experience. We knew down deep inside Satan had tried to destroy our church, but God's power in us was far greater than Satan or any of his demons.

1 John 4:4 (NKJV)
You are of God, little children, and have overcome them, because He who is in you is greater than he who is in the world.

They had to flee when we commanded them to leave in the precious name of Jesus. That is one lesson we learned very well, right from the beginning! It was a very hard thing to watch happen, but it was also a way God let us know He was serious about this church. We knew He had plans, and no one was going to stop Him.

For me personally, moving to the little church was very exciting but also kind of bittersweet. Since I had no money, I had put off going to the doctor. When I was three months pregnant, I finally was able to go to a doctor. I found out my AT&T insurance covered the pregnancy because I had become pregnant when I had the coverage. My first doctor's visit was not good. The doctor checked me out and found everything was fine except I was on a medication known for causing "Hydrocephalus" babies (water head) and babies who were not formed correctly. He started screaming at me and telling me how stupid I was for not going to a doctor for the first three months of my pregnancy. He basically told me he had no hope for this baby to be normal, and I felt like he didn't really want me as a patient. I was in shock and felt like I had done the unfathomable. *How could I have not checked to see what the side effects of my new medicine for headaches were?* I didn't remember seeing anything about not getting pregnant while taking this medicine.

From then on, I avoided telling anyone I was pregnant. I tried to not talk about it. Dan was so mad to find out I was pregnant, he screamed and accused me of tricking him. Now, with this news, he nearly lost it! He screamed out, "That's just what I need now, a retarded baby!" I felt so alone. I remember crying and just believing during the whole pregnancy the baby would be okay. I just couldn't believe my baby would not be okay. Somehow, I felt down deep inside everything was going to be fine. For some reason, I felt a peace about it, even in the middle of all this turmoil. I had trusted God too many times before, and He had never failed me. Surely He would take care of me now. I never did feel like God was preparing me for a deformed baby. He seemed to just give me peace and ask me to trust Him.

I went to the second doctor only to receive the same news. He didn't scream at me, but he did tell me what to expect at delivery. I was scolded again for not checking on the medicine I was taking at the beginning of my pregnancy. However, he was much kinder to me and didn't act like I was an idiot. I was three and a half months pregnant at that time. The only thing I could do now was try to be healthy the rest of the nine months. I cried during the whole pregnancy. Everything upset me—the new surroundings, my hormones, I was 1000 miles away from my family and friends, and I just felt lonely. My mother tried to get me to come back home, even though she didn't know I was pregnant. Somehow, I just knew I was supposed to stay there and everything was going to be okay. I just trudged on, trying to be tough and do what I knew was right. God continued to assure me I was in the right place, and He was in charge. It didn't make it easy, but it made it possible to endure all I went through.

Another terrible problem we had was our home. The mobile home next to the church was our parsonage. It was nice, but it was also roach infested. Every pest control company we called couldn't kill the roaches. They had infested the walls of the mobile home while it sat empty. They just couldn't get rid of them. They were so bad we would open the door before we came in, switch on the light, shut the door again to let the bugs get out of sight, open the door again and then go in. That way we didn't see how dark the floor was as it was covered by roaches. I finally accepted I couldn't get rid of them and I had to live with them. It wasn't easy, but I had no choice. God wouldn't give me more than He and I could handle. I knew that.

God continued to assure me I was in the right place, and He was in charge.

There was also a leak in the mobile home roof, right above my piano. It warped the wood on my piano, so eventually we painted the piano an antique color to make the warped place not show as much. We had to put a lot of our furniture in storage (which wasn't secure by any means) in a barn close by. I don't think we ever were able to use the stored items again. There were no storage places in town. I don't think they had ever heard of one. It seemed to me we had stepped back twenty years in time. We just took it all one step at a time and got through it. It all seemed worthwhile when we saw the faces of all the new Christians and their families coming to church. Their lives were changed forever, and that was worth everything we had to endure.

By my seventh month of pregnancy, everyone could tell I was pregnant, so I quit hiding it. I just told them my due date was December 10. No one needed to know all the doomsday predictions the doctors had made. At Thanksgiving, we were invited to have dinner with the Matthews family. Hannah cooked a big dinner, and, after we ate, I began to feel very ill. I asked if I could lie down, and they fixed me a place. I became much worse, so we finally just went on home. I remember lying on the bed dreaming Hannah was mad at me because I couldn't help her clean up Thanksgiving dinner. She had worked so hard to cook; the least I could do was help clean up. I think I felt guilty but was just too sick to do anything about it.

I vomited all evening and into the night. Finally, at dawn, I called my doctor. He wanted me to come to his office around noon. A friend was taking me to the doctor's office, but on the way, I told her to please just take me to the hospital. I was really sick, and I felt like I was having the baby. She did as I asked and checked me into the closest hospital. The doctor walked in to the room very mad, and he told me I had wasted everybody's time and money by coming because he thought I just had the flu. No one had checked me yet, and I wasn't due until December 10. I was too sick to argue. He finally decided to check me since I was there. It was then he realized I not only had the flu, but I was also having the baby. He put me in a room immediately!

I was so relieved the doctor finally believed me! It was only two or three hours before I delivered my first, live baby girl! The doctor told me it was a very difficult delivery, but I didn't know it because they gave me a spinal block. Sarah was born at 1:30 p.m. and weighed 9 lbs. 4 oz. I guess I was too sick to get nervous or worry about anything. All I remember is the doctor told me I had a perfect little girl, and he held her up so I could see her. I couldn't believe my eyes. She was perfectly formed—a beautiful baby girl! I think I passed out then and slept. It was a wonderful day to know my baby girl was okay. Again, God did not disappoint me. He rewarded me for trusting Him against all odds! It was so exciting to have another baby. Dan only wanted two children, but God didn't agree with that decision. He knew I wanted more children and also a girl. I was so glad God agreed with me. He gave me a perfectly healthy baby girl. What a miracle!

Because of my hard delivery and my having the flu during delivery, I was very weak when it was time to go home from the hospital. I was in bed for nearly two weeks before I got enough strength to stay up and take care of my children. The church was so good. They hired a nanny to stay with me and the children. She was such a help. I know I couldn't have made it without her. A church in a city close by had a shower for me, so we had all we needed to make it.

I remember learning more than one lesson about healing while we pastored in this small community. These lessons stayed with me for the rest of my life. My children had the flu, and they were passing it from one to the other. Then back again to the first one. It seemed it would never end. I was worn out from taking care of them one right after the other. I sat down thinking, *"I can't do this much longer. I am worn out."* I heard a voice say, *"You haven't even asked Me to heal them."* All at once I thought, *"No, I haven't even asked God to help us."* I immediately said, "God, please heal my children from this flu." Right then, the flu went away and never came back. I realized, *"So many times I try to handle everything myself. Then, when I am at the end of myself, I turn to God. I waste so much energy and time. Why don't I ask God to help when the problem arises, not when I am worn out and ready to collapse?"* He is there, waiting for me to just ask. What a lesson!

Matthew 7:7–11 (NKJV)

"Ask, and it will be given to you; seek, and you will find; knock, and it will be opened to you. For everyone who asks receives, and he who seeks finds, and to him who knocks it will be opened. Or what man is there among you who, if his son asks for bread, will give him a stone? Or if he asks for a fish, will he give him a serpent? If you then, being evil, know how to give good gifts to your children, how much more will your Father who is in heaven give good things to those who ask Him!"

After a year of living in our trailer home, we moved into a rent house for about six months, and then the church at that point was able to buy a three-bedroom parsonage. What a joy that was! We finally had a nice house to live in with plenty of room, a big backyard and *no roaches!* It was a wonderful feeling to see the church grow and be able to purchase a parsonage as well as pay a pastor a living wage. By that time, we were making $120 a week with a nice parsonage, and utilities and insurance were paid for us. We felt like we had weathered the storm and come out on top.

I was beginning to think I could be happy if we had to stay there for a long time. It was feeling like home after only two years. I had adapted to all of the things that seemed so weird at first. The people were like family, and I was excited to see the church flourish like it was. We were winning all of the small church awards for growth and improvement, etc. We even had a great revival service and saw much spiritual growth, and the church was doing quite well. Our musicians came from a city nearby. They fell in love with us, and we fell in love with them. It was a wonderful time of fellowship and services as well. We had visitors from churches close by, too.

One day, out in the yard, Mrs. Williams told me she was really happy about how the church was growing, but she was afraid Dan was preaching so well another bigger church would try to take him. I was a little surprised at her comment. I hadn't really thought about it; however, soon afterward, we did start getting offers to pastor other churches. We had already received an offer to co-pastor our little church and the big Baptist church near us. Then we received a call to go back to our home state as well as go to another church in Louisiana. It was not easy for me to talk about leaving. I even told Dan we could stay there and keep building that church. Why go somewhere else and start over?

Chapter 9

Humble vs. Prestigious

Soon, Dan did receive a call to pastor another church, in a much larger city. Many state-wide functions were held in the church. It was also the home church of the musicians we had used for our revival services. We were excited to go and meet with them again. This church was a very prestigious church. The parsonage was beautiful with two living areas, a formal dining area and a big fenced-in backyard. It all seemed so perfect for our family. Plus, they offered us exactly twice the salary we had been making. Talk about a raise! That was a raise! We would have no financial problems there, and Dan could concentrate on pastoring and preaching. I could stay home and take care of the kids. It was like a dream come true. We could hardly believe it! As we packed our things and drove to our new neighborhood, I remember thinking, *"I feel like the Beverly Hillbillies moving into such a nice neighborhood."* It was so different from our little community! The city was a little more like home, yet still in the south.

Church leaders came to the door regularly, and I was expected to take the lead in Women's Groups, board meetings and the music program. After a short time, I became Dan's secretary—mainly because no one else could satisfy him. It took about two years for him to finally find someone he could work with. While we were pastoring there, Dan became very involved in Youth Camp as well as the Youth Outreach Team and other area activities. Our lives were so different! Dan was gone quite often, and I was very busy with the children and church responsibilities.

I became the church organist immediately after our first Sunday morning service. The couple, who had been the singers and musicians for our revival earlier, were the pianist and organist in our new church. As Dan and I greeted everyone at the door, after our first Sunday morning service, this couple came

God always knows what's ahead and prepares us if we'll listen to Him.

by to shake hands and to let us know they would not be coming back! They never gave a reason of any kind, just that this was their last service. They let me know I would probably have to be the church organist since no one else was qualified. It was quite a shock, to say the least, but there was nothing we could do to change their minds. So, once again I became the church organist. This job took quite a lot of my time with practices and services; however, there really was no one else in the congregation who could handle the job. It was a very beautiful organ, and I truly did enjoy playing it. I was reminded of how I had earlier been encouraged to take organ lessons and learn how to play. I was so glad I had felt inclined to do that. God always knows what's ahead and prepares us if we'll listen to Him.

A few weeks after we arrived at our new church, Daniel had an accident on his little bicycle, which still had training wheels on it. A neighbor pulled into his driveway, right in front of Daniel as he rode his bicycle down the sidewalk. Daniel was thrown forward and the bicycle severed his urethra tube. He came in the door with blood running profusely down the front of his jeans; they were soaked in blood. Dan came in the door just as I realized I needed help. He carried Daniel to the car and went straight to the emergency room. In the ER, there just happened to be the best Urologist in the city. He operated immediately, with no sedative, and reattached the urethra tube. It was a very painful procedure, and Daniel screamed and cried so pitifully Dan started to pass out and had to be removed from the room. So, all during the surgery, Daniel cried and screamed that they were killing him as Dan sat outside the door and listened. I finally got a babysitter for Mark and Sarah and got to the hospital as they were finishing the surgery. I sat in that hospital room for eight days and nights with Daniel, listening to him scream and cry with pain. He couldn't understand why God wouldn't stop the pain. I couldn't either, but I had to believe God was there, even though we couldn't feel it.

When someone would try to pray, Daniel would scream, "There's no God. He doesn't hear me!" It broke my heart. He was only six years old, and we couldn't convince him God was there. He didn't understand any of it. It was one of the hardest things I have ever gone through in my entire life. It was eight days of pure torture for Daniel as well as for me. I was so thankful when the pain finally subsided and we could go home. I was totally exhausted and emotionally drained. This experience was one I had to just leave with God. I knew I had done all I could do, and I had to trust God with it. Why He didn't take away the awful pain from Daniel, I don't know. I was quite sure God sent Dan home at precisely the right moment to get Daniel to the hospital quickly. I also knew God had placed the best Urology surgeon in the area at the hospital ER at the right moment to operate. The rest I had to trust God for. Daniel did quite well after the surgery. The doctor thought he might have to have a second surgery, but he didn't need it. He healed quickly and never had another problem. For some reason, we went through that horrific experience. I still do not know why, but I continue to leave it with the One Who does. I trust Him totally with my children.

After this hospital experience, we went back to our busy lives at the church and at home with the children. Dan began to find the new church board was not as easy to work with as the one at our previous pastorate and the people here in our new church were not all quite as willing to accept new members as we had imagined they would be. There was a struggle between the old and new constantly. New people didn't get the love and respect they should have received because of the jealousy and self-righteousness coming from the older members. It was so obvious to us this was not what God wanted. We wondered how a mature Christian could not want to build God's Kingdom? How could they not allow new Christians to come to our church and take a place of leadership and grow spiritually? Why would an older member expect a new Christian to just attend our church and not want to take part in it? Had they forgotten how they felt as new Christians? The very excitement of becoming a new Christian causes a person to want to do everything they can to build God's Kingdom, including serving at the church.

The new Christians had all the enthusiasm in the world, but the older members would put them in their places and stop them from doing anything.

One new lady wanted to just invite all of the elderly people over to her home on their birthdays. She would have a very nice birthday supper and give each one a present. She just wanted to make their birthday a special occasion for them—and it did. The elderly members loved it. Can you believe some of the older members decided this new lady was not spiritual enough to be doing anything in "OUR CHURCH"? They didn't want her to make people think she was a representative of "OUR CHURCH" because they thought she wore too much makeup and didn't act quite like they thought she should. Actually, I think they were jealous of her and the affection she was getting from all of the elderly people in our church who had been ignored for so long. It was such a sad thing to watch! It broke my heart.

These same ladies made a rule no one could serve with silver at our Adult Fellowships. They wanted everyone to serve on paper because it made some people look bad who didn't have silver. It was so obvious they merely didn't want to be outdone. If a new person had silver and wanted to use it at our Adult Fellowships, why in the world couldn't they do that? I always felt like they were letting us know how special we were to them. These ladies basically ran off new, well-to-do, highly educated families we had visiting our church.

Also, they did not make less fortunate families feel welcome either. They snubbed their noses at the clothes of the very poor or those who didn't dress properly. They wanted "THEIR CHURCH" to be a prestigious church where *they* were the leaders. No one below their social class or above it was a welcome member. Or should we say no one who really wanted to get involved was welcome. They would tolerate them just coming to service, sitting on a bench; however, if they volunteered to help with something, they were severely scrutinized and basically boycotted.

We had one non-Christian man who came with his Christian wife and children, wearing flip flops to every service just to irritate the snobby members who didn't want him there. He actually admitted that to us a few years later. How sad to be a part of that. Of course, the church could only grow so much. Most people want to become a real part of their church, not sit on the sidelines and watch other people do everything. They like to give their ideas and feel like they are part of a church family. That just didn't happen in this church. It was so, so sad.

One incident happened while we served at this church that has always stuck in my mind. I never did find out why it happened or if I even knew the person involved. I had just turned out my bedroom light and was getting into bed when my phone rang. Dan was away at Youth Camp, and I was at home alone with the two smallest children. Dan always took our oldest son, Daniel, with him each year to the camp. Daniel was still a grade school child, but he loved going with his dad to the big kid's camp. The teenagers made over him, and he felt very important since he was the Camp Director's son.

As I picked up the phone and said, "Hello," I heard a very strange voice on the other end of the line. "I am watching you. I know your husband is out of town, and I just saw you turn off your lights. I would like to come in." I remember being so scared I started shaking. I hung up the phone and immediately called the police. I also called the camp where Dan was staying. Someone in the Rec Hall answered and sent my son Daniel to find his dad. Soon Dan came home to see what was happening. He was fortunately only about ten miles away. As Dan came in the door, I was sitting on the edge of the bed with his gun in my hand. I was so afraid I don't think I could have shot it if I needed to. The police came, and we talked about what happened. After the police left, Dan finally left, and I calmed down enough to go to bed and sleep. I never heard anything from the person again. I just asked Dan to please never announce from the pulpit again that he was going to be out of town. That might stop the person from knowing when I was home alone. It was a terrifying night. I never wanted to go through that again.

After serving there for a couple of years, I decided to go home for a visit with my parents. My grandmother was in the early stages of Alzheimer's, but the disease was progressing quite rapidly. I took my children and drove home for a visit. It was a long drive, but we really wanted to go. Dan had too much to do and couldn't go, so I went alone. My mother and father were under quite a burden at that time. My brother's little girl had been found on the street and turned over to Child Services while my brother was stationed in California. His wife wasn't interested in taking care of their daughter anymore. She left her at a babysitter's house and never picked her up. The babysitter couldn't handle her and the other children, so she got away and was roaming the streets when Child Services picked her up. My mother and father became her guardians until my brother could get a hardship leave to come home and care for her.

At this same time, my grandmother was getting so much worse, it took a lot of my mother's time to watch after her. I could easily see my mother was about to break from all the stress and tension. I offered to take my niece to live with me until my brother could decide what to do. I wasn't sure how long before he would be able to take care of her. My mother misunderstood my motives and accused me of trying to hurt her. She started crying and having chest pain. My dad thought my mother was having a heart attack and blamed me for everything. He told me I was killing my mother. I was dumbfounded! How could my offer to help my family have turned into this? I left there in total confusion and shock.

On the drive home, I felt very confused and very hurt. I tried to keep driving just to get home as quickly as possible. I knew I was tired, but I pushed myself very hard. I needed to get away from all the mess of confusion and misunderstanding and get back home where I felt a sense of normality. I drove until about 2:00 a.m. before I finally reached our home. I unloaded the children, suitcases, etc. Then I fell asleep until morning. The next morning, I woke up, got in the

I felt absolutely no emotion for one whole year.

shower and felt myself passing out. I grabbed the walls of the shower as I fell to the floor. I didn't hit my head; I just blacked out. Dan heard something strange, so he came to check on me. He got me out of the shower and took me immediately to the ER. They admitted me to the hospital where I lay asleep for eight days! They ran every test possible but found nothing wrong. I remember hearing people come into my room but thinking, *"I'm too tired to open my eyes."* I just needed to rest. After eight days, I finally started waking up. The doctor came in and told me I had an "emotional breakdown." He said, "If you ever do this again, you won't come out of it. This time it was very close."

I felt absolutely no emotion for one whole year. I knew I loved and that I was loved but I couldn't *feel* love of any kind. I knew I loved God but felt no emotion for, or from, Him either. From then on, I had to be very careful to watch my emotions. If I was getting too upset or too tired, I had to back off. I wanted to be around to raise my family, so I had to avoid allowing myself to become very emotional ever again. As the years passed, I learned more and more about how to do this. I talked to myself and had to totally trust God with everything. If I couldn't understand it, I had to just leave it with God. I wasn't able to share anything spiritual with my parents, but that wasn't easy to do because I wanted to be close to them. I finally had to accept the fact they might never understand my relationship with God and that my heart was truly pure in its motives. God knew it, and that's what really mattered. One day, God would make it all okay. I had to leave it with the One who does understand me.

Throughout the years, I realized my niece was probably my mother's only escape from losing her mother to Alzheimer's. It is such a terrible disease and very hard for family members to deal with. When your mother doesn't even know who you are, it does something to you you can't explain. It caused my mother to be very unreasonable and nervous. I don't know if she realized how I felt. She was just trying to survive herself. My parents finally had to put my grandmother into a nursing home because they were no longer able to care for her.

Meanwhile, the church was doing very well, and Dan became very good friends with our District Leader. He even jogged several miles a day with him each morning for many months. The man told Dan he was very intrigued with his preaching skills as well as his ability to lead. He told him he could see him taking his job one day. He also commented that he felt Dan was capable of pastoring a much larger congregation. He was ready to put him in a district job very soon. He needed Dan's skills to help at the district level. Of course, Dan was thrilled and began to look forward to new opportunities. I was not at all happy with the news. I was feeling he was away from home too much already. He sometimes traveled with the District Leader just to keep him company. We heard he was even being nicknamed the Assistant DL. I just told Dan I'd pray about it, but I wasn't sure he needed an extra assignment. I was home alone most of the time with our three small children as it was. If he took on more work, we'd never see him.

During our time there, of course, Dan did take on district jobs; however, when he ran on a ballot for an elected office, he did not win. He lost by one vote. He accused me of praying too much that he would not win the election. I didn't pray against him; I just prayed "God's will would be done." I didn't feel Dan should be placed in any more jobs. We hardly saw him as it was.

During our four years in this assignment, I did meet one lady who changed my life forever. She reminded me of my grandmother. Her devotion to God stood out so vividly. She was very friendly and kind to everyone, but she never got really close to other women in the church. Her name was Gloria. Her husband, Pete, who had been in the Air Force, retired and decided to open up a muffler shop. So they moved to town and attended our church regularly. For some reason, they became very determined to stay in that church and to be there with their family at all services and activities. Pete was even elected to serve on the church board.

Pete had been a pilot in the Air Force, and he and Gloria were quite intelligent people, as were their children. They were socially *at least* equal and maybe above the other members of our church. I noticed no clique or whispering behind her back caused Gloria to back up. She went on, as if nothing hindered her. She loved God with all her heart, and it was obvious to everyone nobody could come between her and her God. Her prayers were so simple, and it was as if she was speaking directly to Jesus. Her testimonies were so sweet and sincere. She acted as if she noticed nothing going on around her. It was just all about her God and her family. Gloria, her husband and her children were all very close. They always stood together and were always unaffected by what other people were doing. She became the church pianist, but she let it be known she would give the job to anyone who wanted to do it. She had very little confidence in her piano playing, even though she played quite well.

I watched Gloria for four years; she was always the same. She shared a relationship with God that caused me to long to be closer to Him. I saw something in her I knew pleased God. I recognized that same exceptional relationship with God in her life as I had seen in my Grandmother's. In my entire life, these are the two people who stood out so much! I felt sure they knew God and loved Him with all their hearts. It was an inspiration to me to seek God and to find Him as they had. I think meeting Gloria made this whole experience all worth it for me.

Several times during our years in this church, Dan became very discouraged and even mentioned he might quit preaching. He even looked for a secular job for a while. Each time, he would quit looking and keep trying to get excited about the church he pastored. It got very old, and finally, he got tired of fighting the old members. The church actually doubled in size while we were there, but it was an uphill battle all the way. We had to stay close to the new people just to be sure they didn't give up and leave.

Dan eventually decided to resign and move on to a church that wanted to grow and see people saved and truly discipled. He began looking for another church to pastor. I have to admit, pastoring in this very prestigious church helped us financially, but it was a hard assignment. It was like being in a very hard class for four years. I longed for the days of working with a group of people who were truly excited about serving God and willing to do whatever it took to win new people to the Kingdom! We might have been poor in finances previously, but we were rich in so many other ways. We yearned to be in a church that was excited about new Christians.

Chapter 10

Heading Straight into the Storm!

Soon, we received an invitation to move to a church in Northern Louisiana. We were ready to move on to a new church and new experiences. As we moved, we actually wondered if we had even made a real difference in that church. We also felt sure many of the new people who came there while we pastored the church would probably move to another church where they felt more welcome.

Our next church assignment was a very interesting experience. If Dan had thought he had a stormy four years previously, he ran into a two-year hurricane in our new assignment! It was an experience I personally never want to go through again.

As soon as we arrived, we felt a tension between us and one of our main leaders and board members. He was waiting to see what type of leadership Dan would provide—before he divided the church! When he saw Dan was planning to be the leader of the church and he would not be leading, he took his family and several others and left the church. This transpired about two or three months after we arrived. Of course, we were shocked and hadn't had much time to establish ourselves before it happened. Basically, the church divided in half. The division left the church devastated and morale was very, very low. It also left the church unable to pay its monthly financial obligations.

The first thing we did was try to get ourselves in a place financially so we could take a major salary cut. Dan got a job driving a school bus so he could be at the church during most of the daytime hours and weekends. He could also be off work during the summer and available to work at the Youth Camp as he had been doing for several years. I worked at AT&T as I had done on previous occasions. We were able to do fine financially—ourselves. The church, however, struggled to survive. Though we worked hard to bring the church out of the devastation, it continued to be very low in morale and grew very little in the two years we were there.

It was hard on me to work full-time, take care of my children, play the organ at church and do anything else I needed to do to keep the church going. I felt bad about not being able to help more, but I knew my limits. I had to be a wife and mother first, so the church had to take third place. During those two years, Dan moved my parents and his sister, Sandra, and her husband down to help us. It was good to have family close by, but the church still did not take a positive turn. No matter how hard everyone worked, nothing seemed to go right at the church.

One evening, after coming home from a Wednesday night prayer service, Dan came in the door very upset. He asked where Daniel was. He said Daniel had told one of the board member's children his dad was looking at a Playboy magazine. He took Daniel back to our bedroom, and I could hear him hollering at him. The whole experience seemed very odd, but I thought maybe Daniel was just showing off to the other boys. He was twelve now, and the boys were starting to talk about sex. Maybe he wanted to shock them. I was surprised Daniel would say such a thing. My mother was at our house when it happened. Both of us kind of brushed it off as Daniel doing a childish thing and thought that Dan would explain to him why he couldn't talk about those things to other children. Daniel had been a very good child up to this point. He was very good and didn't lie as far as I knew. I thought maybe this was one of the signs he was getting close to being a teenager. I had hoped to not have those problems with Daniel. We were very close, and he was such a sweet kid.

There were a few good things that happened while we pastored there. I enrolled our children in a private church school across town. They all began to excel in the private church school program. Daniel's improvement was the most noticeable. He began to do exceptionally well. I was very proud of him. The public schools our children had been attending were known for being some of the worst in the U.S. Our kids needed an extra boost. I was very excited to give them a chance to get caught up academically. They were also taught Bible and Christian principles in the private school, which really helped.

It gave the children more friends and put them in a good church atmosphere. Since our church had such low morale because of the split, it was a very good experience for our family to be connected to a very healthy church. My mother even volunteered as a teacher's helper at the children's school, which made them very excited.

It was also one of the few times in their lives my children lived by their grandparents, aunt, uncle and cousins. Grandpa always invited one child each week to go out to dinner with him and Grandma (always to Luby's Cafeteria). Of course, that was a major event. Also, the kids could go over to Grandma's any time they wanted to and be spoiled. They all loved that, especially when I was at work during the evenings. They were also able to get to really know Aunt Sandra and her husband while we were there. It was so unusual for us to be surrounded by family.

Not long after we were in our new pastorate, I came home one evening to find Dan had purchased a VHS player for our TV. I didn't know a lot about this brand new technology, but Dan seemed to think it was great. He had gone in debt to purchase this new piece of equipment. I wasn't happy about that, but he had already made the purchase. It never mattered what I thought anyway. Soon, Dan was playing around with the VHS player and other equipment he found at the church. I had no idea what he was doing. He seemed to enjoy it, so I didn't complain anymore. We were able to make the payments since I was working and he was driving the school bus. All I knew about it was that Dan was recording things on one machine and putting them on the other. I was not at all talented in the technical field. Dan spent hours on the new machine.

One evening, we had a scare I will never forget. Daniel, Mark and Sarah were playing out in the carport, and it got dark. Dan was inside watching TV or something on his VHS player. He often forgot everything else when he focused on TV. The neighborhood teenagers had come over, and they were all playing in the carport when a figure with a mask came out of our bushes and picked Daniel up (he was 12 at the time). The person started running toward the road. At first, Daniel and everyone there thought the person with the mask was one of the other teenagers in our neighborhood just playing a joke. It didn't take long for Daniel to realize he didn't know the person carrying him. He smelled cigarettes on their breath, and no one Daniel knew smoked. Just as the person got to the street where he had left his car, another car pulled up in the street and stopped, shining their lights right on Daniel and the person in the mask. The masked person became scared. He dropped Daniel and ran for his car. He took off in his car very quickly, and Daniel ran back to our house.

I knew God was watching out for my children.

All at once, it dawned on everyone the masked man had been trying to kidnap Daniel! The mysterious car that had stopped and shone its lights on them had saved Daniel's life. The children ran inside and told Dan what had happened. He was very shook up. I don't think he ever got over the fact he almost lost his son to a kidnapper while he was supposed to be watching him. It was very traumatic for all of us. I knew God was watching out for my children. I was so thankful for Him sending the mysterious car and proving to me once again He truly was taking care of my family—even when I was not there.

Finally, in the fall of our second year there, Dan began to act very strange during the Sunday evening service. He started crying and turned to his brother-in-law looking very confused. He couldn't finish his sermon, so church was dismissed, and he made an appointment to see a doctor right away. I was quite sure he was having a nervous collapse. His confusion was quite bad. After much testing, the doctor turned Dan over to a psychologist for counseling. He was in counseling for several months.

He took a little time off from preaching, at least until he could get his thoughts together. During the time Dan was in counseling, he brought home an XXX Rated VHS movie. He told me his doctor had recommended he watch some of these movies because he was so mixed up about sex. I watched a little of the movie with him at his request but finally told him I couldn't watch this kind of movie. It was extremely pornographic! The movie made me feel very dirty and almost sick. I told Dan in my judgment this was not good for anyone. This wasn't something make-believe; these were real people. They were not dolls or cartoons; they were actual people performing these terrible acts in person. Watching this was the same as committing adultery as far as I could see. Lusting after a person in a movie was no different than lusting after a person standing right in front of you. I didn't see the difference. The sin takes place in your mind and heart whether you physically are able to act upon it or not. I couldn't understand how this type of movie could actually help anyone.

Of course, Dan disagreed with me. He acted as though I was unreasonably conservative, and I had no comprehension of what he'd been through as a child. He insisted that watching these XXX Rated movies could help him get straightened out in his head as far as sex was concerned. I felt these movies could really cause anyone to become distorted about their ideas of marital sex, but I was fighting against Dan and his doctor. So, I decided to do my best to ignore the fact that he was watching these movies when no one else was around. I began to notice he was watching those movies very often.

I was basically caught between my own beliefs and what a certified psychologist was telling Dan to do. I was concerned his breakdown could have happened because of his confusion about many things. If sex was one of these things, I didn't want to make him worse. So, even though I felt strongly this was the wrong therapy, I had little control over Dan's decision to continue. He seemed to like the psychologist. At that time, I was in my thirties and not well-informed about the different types of therapy. Later, I heard this type of recommendation was made by several psychologists during that period of time. Then they realized it was not beneficial. Actually, it was very harmful to many people. I feel Dan was definitely one of them.

Dan also told me his psychologist recommended he try sex with someone different. It could be anyone—even a prostitute! The doctor felt he had been sheltered in our conservative religious beliefs for so long his mind had gotten warped. His natural desires were being squashed, and it was causing him to be very confused about himself. These beliefs were those of his mother as well as those of our church. The doctor recommended Dan get out of the preaching field and do something he could actually be in agreement with. The church's beliefs were confusing him too much. I disagreed totally but could not convince Dan the doctor was wrong.

Since this subject was so confidential, I didn't know who else to talk to about it. I told no one what was going on. I think my mind basically was either in a type of shock or complete denial of the situation. I was working full-time, trying to continue to play the organ at the church, keep the children in school and making sure their homework was completed each evening. Then I had Dan and his doctor telling me I was making the situation worse with my conservative beliefs. My heart was heavy because I couldn't believe any differently. I knew I was right. When I prayed, I felt more than ever Dan was receiving very harmful counsel, but he totally disagreed, so my hands were tied. I couldn't make him stop the counseling.

I was asked to come in and talk to Dan's doctor just one time. He questioned me for about 15 to 20 minutes. At the end, he made one statement: "I don't know how you and Dan have stayed married for 18 years. You are too different." I knew from his statement he had no intention of taking me on in an argument. He just felt Dan and I were very mismatched.

When Dan said he was ready to go back to pastoring the church, he was still not himself. After he went back, he told me he was going to have to get out of preaching for a while. I was in agreement with him at this point. After what I'd just been through, I knew he had no business preaching. He was not acting like a preacher. All I could do was pray for him. As we began making plans to move, Dan received a call from the head of a church in Arkansas. He invited us to consider moving to a church in a small farming community in Arkansas. To my surprise, Dan began to act like his old self again. He became enthusiastic and excited and talking about what he could do in the Arkansas church. I couldn't believe the transformation! I asked him if he was sure he could do this, and he assured me he wanted to try. I was shocked he would even consider pastoring another church so soon. It was as if an immediate healing took place when he received that phone call. He acted so completely changed, I began to think this craziness was over. Dan was back! He finally realized the church and its beliefs were right after all. This counseling and this bad doctor would be just a bad memory of the past. I was so thankful for the change. We made plans to move as soon as school was out for the summer. I began to feel like I had lived through one of the biggest nightmares of my life. I wanted to put this behind us as quickly as possible.

As we pulled the moving van out of our driveway, several people came to say goodbye. We did make several lifelong friendships in that church, in spite of the many problems we had. A few people were really sad to see us leave. I felt so sorry for a little, dark haired, 13-year-old girl who had helped babysit our children when I was at work. She stood there looking so sad, almost in tears. I will never forget that look on her face. I couldn't believe how hard she was taking our move. She looked so lost; it was almost a hopeless look on her face. I felt bad we had to leave her like that. My heart went out to her. I hadn't realized how she felt and hadn't been able to talk to her before we left. Those eyes never left my memory. Even to this day, I see her standing in our driveway, looking so lost. As we left, and since then, I have wondered if we helped or hindered the church there. I know our children were better off for having gone to the Christian school, but as far as the church went, I don't know if we helped it or not.

Chapter 11

Joy vs. Frustration

We moved to Arkansas in the spring of 1983 (all of our family who had been helping us in Louisiana came, too) and became very busy as soon as we arrived. The parsonage was right across the street from the school. I had kids playing at my house and in my yard continuously. My children constantly brought friends home to feed. I felt this was a good place to raise our children at that time in their lives. They were surrounded by friends, country and hardworking, good people who really did love them very much. Our new community was like a big family—especially our church. Old and young alike became good friends of ours. We woke up in the summer time with baskets of food on our doorstep. I learned to freeze, can and cook many new dishes. These farm people provided well for us, and it was so different from life in the big city. We all really loved it.

The church was a little backward from what Dan had been used to, but he began to realize how to move along with them. He was able to lead them in building a brand new church with a beautiful sanctuary, a gymnasium for the youth, Sunday school classrooms, a nice office and a warm welcoming entryway. The location was a prime location, and the church could be seen for miles away with its high church steeple. The people were very proud of their new facility. Their old building had been in very bad shape, termite-infested and not at all adequate for a growing church. It took a great deal of hard work, but it was well worth it when we saw our new building finished. Building the new church was not without problems, as is any building program; however, God saw us through it and led us every step of the way. Not once did He leave us alone! The people became very close to us as well as to each other. We truly became a church.

During the building of the church, I realized Dan had begun acting very aloof towards me. He was *very* friendly with another lady who was helping him in the office and didn't seem to really want me around. He even came home

> *I prayed and cried out to God continually just to be able to get through this period of time.*

in the evenings and laughed and giggled with her on the phone for quite some time. I asked him to please try to be less friendly with the lady or people would be talking. His reply was, "You sure don't make me love you more with all of this jealousy." Dan became very spiteful to me, and I knew I had to just keep quiet or suffer the consequences. I felt like I needed to just stay away from the church offices and leave him alone in order to keep peace in our home. I knew he had become emotionally attached, but I did not believe he was having a physical affair.

During this time, I kept thinking about the breakdown Dan had earlier. I felt his mind was so confused he couldn't see what the real problem was. I continued to pray and believe he would come out of this and go back to being himself soon, as he had in our last pastorate. I would just try to get through it. I began to have several types of illnesses during this time: pain in my wrists so I had to wear a wrist brace at night; allergies and asthma began to appear regularly and cause me to be bedfast off and on; and my nerves were very bad, but I did my best to control them. I smiled and tried to be as hospitable as possible to the church people. I didn't want them to know anything was wrong. Dan was causing enough talk without me adding to it.

I also was having a terrible discipline problem with Daniel. It seemed as if I had lost control of him. His dad had started disciplining him more, and Daniel seemed to snub me. He acted like he didn't have to do anything I said. Many times, he even twisted my already hurting wrists when I tried to correct him. He had turned into a very rebellious young man. I prayed and cried out to God continually just to be able to get through this period of time. I knew this was not Daniel's true feelings for me. Every time he was cruel to me, I would tell myself he did not mean what he said. It was just a stage he was going through, and one day he would come out of it. Then I'd have my sweet, loving Daniel back. I couldn't wait for those days to be over. I thought all the horror stories I'd heard about teenagers must be true. And Daniel must be one of the worst!

The church provided counseling for pastors and their wives in another city, which was quite a drive from home; however, I knew I desperately needed help. I decided to go talk to a church counselor. I didn't want anyone to know what I was doing—not even Dan. I kept it very confidential, but he finally figured out what I was doing. He would act very catty when I went for an appointment. It took only a few sessions for me to realize I could not break up our family. My children adored their father, and I knew he had a personality that could sway anyone. The counselor helped me to set limits on how much I could take. For me, it had to be until I knew my children could see the problem and understand enough to agree the marriage was over. Also, I needed them to believe I should not stay with their father and ignore his lack of respect for me anymore. I would stay indefinitely unless my children were in agreement to go with me.

I continued to do my best to keep our home a happy place for all of us. Sometimes, it was very hard, but I knew I had to do it. I kept pushing on, hoping things would get better. I first took a part-time job typing the town newspaper. Next, I took an H&R Block® course and started figuring taxes. I loved that, and it helped keep my mind occupied.

After the church building was finished, Dan became very bored and was feeling a lack of push and drive. He decided to build houses with my uncle who had been the contractor for building our church building. They built a couple of houses, and Dan spent less time at the church. I noticed he became more restless as time passed. It was obvious to me he was not happy. He became very irritable and short-tempered. His house building project was not going as planned and that began to wear on him quite heavily. He needed to borrow more money to keep the business afloat, and he was upset with me for saying we shouldn't be borrowing more money. I tried talking to him, but he wouldn't listen when I told him he just needed to work on the church now that we had a wonderful facility to work with. Somehow, he lost his drive to work at the church, and he began to say he wanted to move on to a new project.

All of us hated to think of moving. The people there had become like family, and the children loved the closeness we felt to the people in the church as well as the town. We had even started a Community Store. We never turned down anyone who needed help. People needing gas, groceries, clothes or a place to stay overnight, just came to our little Community Store, and we always provided whatever they needed: food, clothing, etc., for meager prices like 50¢ or a quarter. Yet, we made a good profit each month from the sales. God really did bless our work in that store, and our church ladies loved working there and helping our community. The whole community loved it, too! How could we just leave all of this and move on? Moving was such a hard thing to do! None of us, except Dan, really wanted to move again. Only one problem really prompted me to want to move.

I knew there were rumors all over town about Dan and the lady in our church. I kept hoping they would die down. I tried to talk to him again about not being so friendly with her, but he was very belligerent when I tried to talk about it. He acted as if he didn't care what people thought, that was their problem—until one day, the lady's husband got word of the rumors. He was furious and put an end to his wife working at our church or seeing Dan for any reason. I believe the couple started having major marital problems because of Dan. The husband was on our church board and had been a very friendly guy who supported Dan completely. After this, the husband wouldn't even look Dan in the face. He turned his head when he passed him and sat in church looking at the floor. It was so obvious what was wrong! I believe several people in our congregation, especially board members, knew what was wrong. It seemed nothing Dan did could make it okay again.

So, with this problem weighing heavily on us, we did start looking for other employment. It was obvious we had to move. At first, Dan looked for a secular job. Then he changed his mind and decided to continue preaching. An evangelist came to hold a revival for us in the fall of 1986. He told us he thought we would be a great match for a church he knew that needed a pastor and asked us if he could give our names to the board there. Dan agreed to check them out and the next thing we knew, we were moving to Texas in December of 1986.

Chapter 12

Mysterious Symbols

I drove the kids back to Arkansas for the remainder of the December semester, which was about three weeks. Then, we all moved right before the Christmas holidays. This time, the rest of our family did not come with us. They were tired of constantly moving.

We liked the people and the new church quite well. The parsonage had five bedrooms and an office. It was a very lovely home, and we settled in quickly. We had one huge problem! We discovered demonic symbols drawn on the inside wall of Mark's closet. The writings were back beyond the closet, in a little hideout type of space, not easily seen. The associate pastor assured us he had prayed over the house many times and had done his best to rid it of any sign of demonic drawing or activity. He told us the previous pastor's grandson had been living there in the parsonage with his grandparents. The grandson was a teenager who had been dabbling in demonic worship.

Since the house had been prayed over, we felt like everything would be fine. At that time, we were pretty ignorant of demons and what to do with them. Our church denomination had very little teaching on this subject. We had no idea what we were in for. Soon after we moved in, Mark started refusing to sleep in his room. He said there were spiders constantly by his bed, and he couldn't get rid of them. We sprayed, but they seemed to always come back. Then one night, Sarah saw a demon in her bedroom. She kept saying the name of Jesus as we had taught her to do. That was the only teaching we had ever heard on getting rid of demons. We were told demons will not stay around when you call on the name of Jesus. Sarah said the demon left as she repeatedly spoke the name of Jesus. We were so glad that worked.

When we had been in Texas for just a few months, we received a phone call from the Police Department a few cities away from us. They asked us to be on the lookout for the former pastor's grandson, Johnny. They felt he was headed our way, and they knew he had lived in our house for quite some time. They said he needed a place to hide, so he might try to get into our house. They told us Johnny had been at a football game one evening with several friends. After the game, he told his friends he was going to go home and kill his grandparents. His grandparents had been hassling him about smoking, and he was tired of it. Of course, the friends thought he was only joking. They laughed and went on home. Soon afterward, the police found the grandparents murdered in their home. The grandmother had been shot in the kitchen, and the grandfather was shot in his bed. They said it was a very gruesome murder scene. The grandparents had been shot several times, and Johnny was missing. The police felt confident he was the gunman.

After Johnny was apprehended at the Mexico border, we heard he was being transported secretly to the city jail where the murder had occurred because they were afraid the local cult members might try to free him. Soon, we heard he had confessed to the murders and was found guilty. He was sentenced to many years in prison. This whole incident caused us to be more alert to what demonic activity meant. We had not been aware of any demonic activity since our first pastorate.

Next, our children all began to complain about the school system. The stories they were telling me each evening after school began to stir something inside of me. *How can I allow my children to be taught this way in school? This is totally against all I believe.* Mark came home several evenings crying and saying, "Mom, you have to get us out of here. Can't you find a Christian School for us?" Our oldest son, Daniel, made the statement: "There is no possible way to be a Christian in this High School." Sarah was devastated over the way the girls had to have name brand clothing. If she didn't wear name brand clothes, they laughed and made fun of her. She was very unhappy with their attitudes and became more reluctant to keep going each day, just as Mark was. I began to pray and ask God what to do.

At that same time, some of the very popular TV evangelists were falling from their faith, and the TV news was showing them on their broadcasts as they made their confessions. One day, as I came in from walking, a televangelist was on the TV, crying and confessing his sin of seeing a prostitute. Dan was in his office, which was right inside the front door. As I came through the door, I noticed he was deep in thought. He seemed almost depressed. As I walked in, he said, "He wanted to get caught. It was a relief to him to be found out. Now he doesn't have to hide it anymore." I looked at Dan and said, "Why do you say that?" He just looked very sad and said he just knew. I thought his answer was very odd. I had never thought about it like that. *Was it true? Had he been careless just so he'd get caught?* I wondered why Dan would think that.

I started praying and fasting! I started prayer walking at 5:00 a.m. every morning and seeking God's will for my children. I felt like Satan was trying to destroy my children right before my eyes! I wondered if I should home school. I started checking out all possibilities. There were no Christian schools for miles—none in the entire city. I got very serious about all that was happening, so I walked every day and prayed desperately for my children and for God to give me a plan to save my family. I walked and prayed more and more as time went on. Before long, I was walking an hour a day and praying until I felt like I could just step right into Heaven.

It was such a wonderful time with God. He became so close during those walks. I hated to even go home each morning. God showed me so many things during that time. For one thing, He asked how much I really loved Him. I knew I truly loved God, but He was asking me how much. I searched my heart and told God I would love Him always, no matter what. As I was searching to find this answer, I somehow felt God wanted me to commit to love Him even if I lost Dan. I told Him I would but begged Him to please not let Dan leave or go back on Him again. But I settled it then: No matter what Dan did, I was going with God, all the way. It was forever decided in my mind that God would always be first, no matter what happened to me. I knew I could trust Him to guide my life and take me wherever He wanted me to go. I just had to trust Him, and I did.

I was walking an hour a day and praying until I felt like I could just step right into Heaven.

81

Chapter 13

You Want Me to What?

As I continued to pray and fast, one morning I woke up to a very loud voice speaking to me. I sat up startled. The voice was saying: *"Start a Christian School."* I thought, *"You want me to what? Surely that's not for me."* So I got up and found Dan standing close by. I asked him, "Did you hear that voice?" He said, "What voice?" I said, "That voice saying, *'Start a Christian School.'*" Dan kind of snickered and said, "No." So I said to him, "We have to start a Christian School." He said, "We? I didn't hear any voice. *You* have to start a Christian School." I was a little overwhelmed with the incident but asked him if he would help me. He said, "Well, of course, but you are the one God told to do it, not me."

I could not get that voice out of my mind. I told God I would do everything I could to start a Christian School if He would just guide me and show me what to do. I began to check out the Christian Schools in the towns on either side of us and went to visit them. I talked to their directors and told them we were considering starting a Christian School. They volunteered to help in any way they could. They even gave me some tips on how to get started and what training I'd need to start a school. I began to get totally involved in getting training and learning all I could about how to start and develop a Christian School. By the fall, I had decided to enroll my children in a Christian School in a nearby city. I would drive there each morning with my children and work all day learning how a Christian School operates. They would let my children attend for free as long as I helped them with their school all year. I monitored a classroom all year and learned about how the school was run. It was a very good school, and they taught me very well. My children also received a better education there than in the local public school system.

At first, it appeared Daniel wasn't going with us to our Christian School. He was a sophomore in high school. He was still having problems getting along with me, and it was hard for me to correct him. I was determined to discipline him even though it meant a major conflict each time. We had started inviting his friends to our home rather than allowing him to go to theirs. We felt we could control what he did and the atmosphere he was in by doing this. By this time, we were very concerned he could get in serious trouble if we didn't watch him carefully. Some of his friends were not trustworthy, and we knew that. At least we could monitor what they did at our home. We couldn't do that if they were away. I made Daniel a main priority in my prayers as I walked and fasted.

I was so thankful God did what I couldn't begin to do.

As the summer passed, Daniel changed his mind and decided he, too, wanted a Christian education. When Daniel announced he wanted to go to the Christian School, Dan looked at me very suspiciously. He said, "I don't know what you had to do to pull this off, but I can't believe you convinced him to go to a Christian School." I knew what had happened. Only prayer and fasting could have saved Daniel from the life he was headed for. God heard the prayer of a desperate mother who wanted to save her son's life from destruction. Again, I was so thankful God did what I couldn't begin to do.

Public education had not been good for Daniel. He was falling behind and knew he needed personal attention. The public school in our previous pastorate had been more concerned with Daniel's football skills, not his education. God answered my prayer by showing Daniel what would be best for him. Football would not get him a diploma. It was a game, not an education.

Before long, we had friends of my children from our church, wanting to go with me to the Christian School. Some parents would not agree to their children changing schools, and some parents thought it was great. One of Daniel's friends wanted to go with us, which we thought was wonderful. We could tell he was headed for trouble if something didn't change; however, his parents did not want him in a Christian School. They were very against the school and voiced their opinion very vocally. Since the friend's mother was on our church board, she caused quite a lot of dissension. In fact, she even came to Dan one day and told him she was very concerned about our boys being friends. She felt our son, Daniel, was not a good influence on her son. She wanted the friendship to end. Her son was no longer allowed to come to our home to visit Daniel. That actually solved some of *our* problems with Daniel. He soon began to spend more time with another friend who was a much better influence on him. The new friend's parents allowed him to go to the Christian School. He was a very fine young man, very moral and very teachable.

As the year progressed, parents began to decide what they thought about a Christian School. I didn't push the starting of a school, but Dan did bring it up to the church board. It was then taken to our governing church authorities, and they turned us down immediately on starting the Christian School. Dan was actually very disappointed, as was I. I told God, "I don't know what to do now. You have to show me." I knew my children were thriving in a Christian School atmosphere and Christian curriculum, but I couldn't go against the church's authority. Dan and I had both seen great changes for the better in our children. They became more secure and self-confident. They even seemed to be more respectful and more interested in the Bible and spiritual things. It was hard to understand why a church would not want to have a Christian School when we could see so many of the advantages for our children and those we were taking with us. But, I had to wait to see what God's next move was.

To my surprise, God knew all along what He wanted to do. He just needed me to be ready. Our church was growing very quickly. It had doubled in attendance in just eighteen months. Our children's program was exploding. We needed new teachers and helpers for the new church year. We also needed more board members and leaders for the church. Dan announced we would be holding our annual church elections in June—just six weeks away. All at once, we found ourselves in the middle of a very tense atmosphere. Older board members were complaining about all the new people and kids taking over their church. I even overheard one lady say, "This place is like a circus with all these kids running around." I was actually quite shocked! I had been so involved in making the new people feel welcome, I hadn't realized some of the older members actually didn't want them there.

About that time, we had scheduled an all-church seminar on "The Covenant Relationship" with a pastor from Dallas. The pastor came with his family for that weekend, and we were expecting a great seminar. On Friday night, we realized some of the older church members and several board members were boycotting the seminar. They were saying this visiting pastor was leaning to the charismatic side, and they did not want to be associated with him. During that entire seminar, only our new members came to hear the tremendous wisdom on the Covenant Relationship. It was a very embarrassing weekend to say the least. We began to realize our church had some very grave issues that needed to be settled.

As our annual church election drew near, tension became so strong that the head of our church in that area called Dan and asked him if he was speaking in tongues. Dan did not speak in tongues and told him so.

More and more accusations started flying, and it became harder and harder to get the old board members to accept our new members. Their attitude was becoming apparent to everyone. Our treasurer told Dan he'd better start spending his time with the people who were paying his check and less with these new people. Next, the board tried to pass a policy that no one could teach a Sunday school class unless they had been a church member for at least five years. Everything they did was aimed at stopping new members from holding any position in their church. They wanted new people to attend, participate in services, pay what they could and leave. They wanted them to have no authority or "say so" about how the church was run. We couldn't believe this was happening again!

Finally, our area leader called us and said he felt we should take a pastoral vote. Even though it wasn't time for a vote, he'd had too many requests from board members requesting that a new vote be taken right away. So, we announced that a pastoral vote would be taken on a certain Sunday. Of course, this day had to be before our annual church elections.

The morning of the elections, I was walking and praying. I heard God speak very clearly to me and say, *"Dan will be voted out this morning, but it is okay. I have a plan."* I was shocked, but I knew when God spoke to me it was something I could count on. So, I got ready for church, got the kids ready and off we went.

As I approached the church, I could see there were a lot more cars in the parking lot than usual. As I walked into the service, I saw that our area leader had surprisingly showed up for this vote as well as many older members who had moved away years ago but still held their membership in our church. There were many people in attendance I had never seen before in the eighteen months we had been there. Tension was very high, and the husband (who was unsaved) of one of the lady board members, was posted at the church door as a greeter. As people came in, he was advising them to "Vote No." How sad! Politics in full motion right in the church!

The area leader asked Dan and I to come to Dan's office. He told us to just hold on, everything would be fine once the vote was taken. He would handle everything that morning. We were just to relax. He also said we were very fortunate to have him, a great man of prayer, there with us. He felt everything was going to be fine.

As the area leader prepared for a vote, he asked if anyone wished to say anything before the vote. One of the church's older members stood up and came to the front. She was a quiet lady in her 60's. She was well thought of by everyone there and a precious saint.

She began to tell the congregation she had been up praying for several hours and God had spoken to her about this election. She stated that this was not just a pastoral vote. This was a vote for the destiny of this church. If they voted "No" today, they were voting to destroy the spirit of their church, and God was not pleased. She begged everyone to please listen to God and not go against what the Holy Spirit was telling them to do. She was obviously very burdened and very sincere in all she said.

After she sat down, the area leader called for a vote of all members. Much to our leader's surprise, Dan was voted out by just one vote. A two-thirds vote was needed for him to stay, and he lacked one vote from getting a two-thirds majority. As the area leader stood up to announce the vote, he was quite shaken. He told the congregation Dan had a month of vacation days coming to him and he would be spending that month in the church parsonage. After that time, he would move to a new location. He told Dan and me in the back of the church that this church was too backward for us. They didn't understand what we were doing. He said we needed to move to a more progressive church. He said, "If you can just hold on, I'll get you out of here." Meanwhile, he wanted us "to just get through this." Then he met with the local church board to discuss plans for the future of their church.

That afternoon, we received a phone call from one of our new members. He asked us to please come to a home that evening at 6:00 p.m. He made the statement that he and several others were meeting for a church service in the backyard. They were no longer going back to the church building where they were not welcome and where Dan had been voted out. They wanted to start their own church where they felt like God was welcome. Of course, we didn't debate about what we should do that evening. We had nowhere to go, and it had been a very tough day. We agreed to go to the backyard service at 6:00 p.m.

As we got out of our car that evening, we were shocked to find 92 people meeting in a backyard to worship God with all their hearts. It was an amazing service, and we left feeling like we knew where God wanted us. The people were not bitter or angry. They just wanted a church where God could meet with His people and where new people could come to find God. They were anxious to serve God without fighting board members who were so prideful and self-righteous.

Of course, the area church leader was informed immediately that we had met with the new group who had left the church that night. In fact, he called us Monday morning very upset that we had met with them. Dan was asked if he planned to continue meeting with the newly found congregation. When he said that he was, he was informed he had two weeks to get out of the parsonage. He would no longer be a licensed preacher in the denomination and would not receive a month's salary as previously promised. That was quite a shock, and it took us some time to digest all that was happening.

One of our oldest, most respected members traveled quite a distance to ask our church leaders to give our new little church a charter as a brand new church. Our denomination's leaders denied the request. Our people were advised to go back to the church building where we had been meeting and worship with the other members for six months. Then they would talk about starting a new church.

We soon found an old house in the middle of downtown. It could be rented and was good enough for us to move into for a temporary place to live. We had to have a very large yard sale, and we were able to collect enough to help us live on for a month. The house had three bedrooms and was quite a bit smaller, but it was sufficient for our needs at the time. We stayed there for only a few months. We never did unpack everything. We lived with boxes piled up all over the house the whole time we were there.

Finally, we found a house on the outskirts of town with three-quarters of an acre of property. It was next to a wooded area which made a very good place for me to walk. I enjoyed living there and spent much time walking and praying. During that time, I had become very ill with gallbladder attacks which happened quite regularly. Neither we nor the church could afford medical insurance for us, so I postponed seeing a doctor. I was hoping to have insurance if I had to get medical help. A nurse friend in our church told me she was sure I was having gallbladder attacks and they were getting pretty dangerous. I waited a little while longer, then realized that the pain, sweats, nausea and weakness from these attacks were more than I could endure. I knew I needed medical attention quickly.

I walked over to the phone, picked it up and started to dial the phone number to get medical insurance. I heard a voice saying, *"You haven't even asked Me to heal you."* I put the phone down and stood there, stunned to think I had forgotten to pray about all this pain. *How could I have been so busy as to forget to pray about such a serious health problem?* I immediately stopped everything and very quietly said, "God if You want to heal me from this gallbladder problem, I will not call about getting insurance. I will trust You to heal me, and I will not call about insurance unless I have another attack." I went on that day with confidence God knew what I needed, and He would take care of me and keep me safe.

I am writing this story 26 years later. I have never had another gallbladder attack since that day. God healed me completely, just as He told me He wanted to. His Grace stepped in even when I forgot to ask Him. He knew I had no money to pay for medical insurance. He is the Great Physician (Jehovah Rapha), and He had already paid the price for my healing at Calvary. I just had to ask Him. He was patiently waiting for me to ask. My faith increased that day as I realized how much God loved me and cared about my health and finances—even when I was so forgetful and didn't remember to ask.

Chapter 14

Starting a New Church and School

No one was willing to go back to the old church building and those people, so we began to look for another denomination to charter our new church. Soon, we found the right one, and they gladly welcomed us as a part of their association. They were a great group of people, and we loved being a part of their association. We became accountable to them, and they became our covering. Our church met in a Health Center right on the outskirts of town until we found a permanent building to meet in. We then remodeled the inside and had it ready for services by August 1988.

Our church grew, and the spirit in it was really good. We attracted people from other places and new people as well. It was obvious God was building our church. That summer, we also laid plans for our Christian School. We opened the doors of the school in August for the full 12 grades. We had 28 students to start with and a full staff—ready to serve God as He led them. We met at 7:00 a.m. each morning for prayer before school started at 8:00 a.m., and we felt God's Presence throughout the entire school each day as we taught our children and worshipped our God. It was a wonderful beginning!

The first year, we hired an experienced principal while I taught Kindergarten and First Grade. I was really excited to see God work and to see how the children grew spiritually. At the end of the year, my students each tested out well above the Second Grade level. So our curriculum was really doing its job. We were thrilled at the reports of our children both academically and spiritually! We began to be recognized by our public school system because of our great academic scores and our effect on the children who attended. We had several public school teachers in our church. Most of them sent their children to our church school. That in itself was a testimony to how God was helping us to succeed with the school.

That year, my grandmother passed away. I took the kids, and we went up for her funeral. Dan chose not to go with us; he said he was too busy. She had been sick for so long, and I had already grieved for so many years, I was glad she was finally with her Savior and her storms of life were over.

By the second year, we were still going strong and had over 40 students. I didn't teach the second year. I became the full-time Administrator. God spoke to me even before the board asked me to be in charge. He made it quite clear to me this was His plan. This was one of the few times God wanted me to be in the forefront, and I knew He did. Running the school was getting to be quite a job. I even had an accountant to keep our books. The finances were getting to be too much for me to handle. I had to spend a great deal of time running the school. Everything was wonderful, and God was blessing us as we served Him daily, teaching and training children for Him. Our 7:00 a.m. prayer meetings became the talk of the town. People came just to be prayed for who needed healing. Word got around God was meeting with us in those prayer meetings, and He was doing miraculous things. He really was! We saw so many miracles happen!

> *God was meeting with us in those prayer meetings, and He was doing miraculous things.*

I knew I wasn't running this school—God was. I found myself saying and doing things that were not my ideas. I found myself disciplining the children by reading Scripture and praying with them (God's ideas). Everything I did was as if I was just the vessel God was using to have His school going. I have never felt so close to God and so in His will as during the time I worked in that school. It was truly a heavenly experience! I was definitely walking with God by my side!

As things were thriving at the church and school, we were notified a cult was meeting outside our city and trying to curse us. They specifically wanted the pastor to fall from grace with God. They were praying against his marriage and the success and growth of our Christian School. I began to notice a black hearse sitting across from our school playground each day, and it would follow me around town as I ran errands. I was not afraid of it at all. I knew the Word says, *"Greater is He who is in you than he who is in the world"* (1 John 4:4, NASB). I trusted God and kept praying for His will to be done in the church and school. I could see Him working continually. Nothing fell; everything continued to grow as God blessed our efforts.

Then, all at once, I began to see Dan slipping. He was taking His eyes off of God and was looking at the material things around him. Not trusting God and getting scared caused him to waver and finally fall prey to the Enemy—just as the cult had wanted. I tried to warn him of what was happening, but he couldn't seem to get himself back up. He was afraid we wouldn't make it financially and his salary wasn't enough for us to live on. I knew it was just Satan harassing him—but to Dan it was very serious.

He began to make plans to work on the side as well as pastor the church. That alone caused the church to begin to suffer. Just as the church and school were at their peak, when everything was doing so good and God was blessing us with miracle after miracle, Dan began to doubt God. He took His eyes off of God and began to look at all the obstacles that could possibly cause us to fail. I don't know if Satan used Dan's tiredness or his lack of time to read the Word and pray to get in. Somehow, he convinced him to fear that God would not provide for us. From then on, Dan could not seem to just trust God. It became evident in his sermons and in his daily life. I kept praying and trying to help him see what was happening, but he refused to listen. He went head-on—right into trouble.

He decided to open a restaurant and run it as well as pastor our church. I knew it was a mistake but couldn't stop him. He spent most of his days running the restaurant and what time was left went to the church. Finally, it began to feel like I was at the church night and day while he was at the restaurant night and day. We were both exhausted and saw each other only in passing.

One morning, as I was showering for the day, a demon appeared to me. This was the first time in my life I had ever seen a demon, face to face, but I recognized it immediately. It appeared right above my head, and it was laughing hideously at me, throwing its head back as it laughed. Cold chills ran all over me. The sound was deafening and the spirit in the air was chilling. I was shocked at first, and then I remembered to call on the name of Jesus. I began to sing: "Jesus, Jesus, Jesus, there's just something about that name ...." I sang the song over and over again until I was sure the demon was gone for good. A sweet Presence came into the room, the laughing was gone and Jesus took control. I have never had a day like that before or since that experience. The name of Jesus truly did rebuke the demon. I had heard that it would, and now I knew from experience it was true. I knew all I needed was "Jesus."

As Dan began to get worse and worse, I began to feel demonic powers all around me. During one of our school's 7:00 a.m. prayer meetings at the church, I began to feel like I couldn't carry this burden of the school, church and Dan by myself. I had no one to talk to or to pray with. I begged God to please send me someone to help me carry this load. It was getting too heavy for me. As the prayer meeting ended, I looked across from me. There was a woman, probably in her late 50's or early 60's looking at me. She stood up and

God ... will move His people around and do miracles just to help us when we're in need.

came toward me. She walked right up to me and said, "I believe God told me you need ministering to. Am I right?" I broke down. Of course she was right. God was right on time—as usual.

Renee owned a Christian bookstore in town. She told me to come down to her store anytime I needed to talk or pray, so I did. She would get someone to cover the store for her, and she would go to the back with me. She even told me how to go through a back entrance if I didn't want anyone to know I was coming there. Renee told me she knew I had a heavy burden, and she wanted to help me pray this through to victory. She said she would never breathe a word to anyone else. Renee and her husband lived in the country. I was welcome to come to their home anytime I needed quiet time or time to be alone and away from everyone. They wouldn't harass me or talk unless I wanted to.

God knew exactly what I needed. I went to that bookstore many times to pray and to open my heart for advice and counsel. I even spent a day or two at their home in the country when I needed to get away and be alone. It was like a haven of rest to me. I thank God continually for Renee. She never failed to give me a scripture or pray for me as I needed it. I felt such a load lift as we prayed together and she rebuked demons from around me and my family. She was truly God-sent. Only God could have found just the right person, at just the right time, to help me with all I was going through. And Renee helped me so much!

One time, I was feeling guilty because I had slammed Dan's leg in the car door accidently because he hadn't moved it when I asked him to. I had been driving down a main highway and saw him and a young lady friend walking in a parking lot of a restaurant. I knew when I saw them Dan had gone there to meet with her. Even though he had been telling me *she* was chasing *him*, I felt very strongly he was lying. I told Dan I was going to go talk to the lady since I felt he was lying to me about why he had been there. He stuck his leg in the car door. I didn't know it was still there when I slammed it shut.

Renee helped me to see I had done nothing wrong. She knew I blamed myself for *way* too much. Her opinion helped me see so many things from the right perspective. Other times, she just listened and prayed as I talked and cried. Renee was not a member of our church, but she was always there for me. She and her husband had come to our church during that time just because God handpicked them to help me. They had previously been members of another denomination but felt God calling them to attend our church for a period of time. She told me she and her husband were just obeying God when He sent them to our church. Until the day God spoke to her about me, she had no idea why she was attending our church. Later, they went back to their previous denomination to serve God. What a great God we serve! He will move His people around and do miracles just to help us when we're in need.

One day, I saw our church board coming in for an unscheduled meeting. They were meeting to discuss a private subject with Dan. He was not aware of the meeting until they called him. The elders were very upset over some rumors going around about Dan and the young lady who was working for him at his restaurant. They had been told he was seen meeting her out in the country one night recently, and they needed an explanation. Of course, Dan tried to smooth it all over and say it wasn't what they thought. I, however, knew they were probably correct in their accusations. My children were also aware something was going on when they were with their dad and this lady as they were working at the restaurant. I tried to talk to Dan about what was going on, but to no avail. He was closed to the subject and assured me that it was my big imagination again. He told me again I was just a jealous wife. I needed to quit watching him and trust him. He knew what he was doing.

Very shortly after that conversation, I learned I truly could *not* trust him at all and things were much worse than any of us thought! The young lady he worked with came to the school one day screaming at me to let her see Dan again for counseling. She said she needed him and begged me to not keep him from her. I told her she did not need him, and she could not have permission to see my husband in counseling anymore. I was concerned her screaming was so loud the children might have heard her, so I tried to quiet her down but couldn't. Finally, she left. I felt sure the teachers knew she was there. We just didn't discuss it. I was not sure what any of them knew or didn't know. I felt it was best to just say nothing.

Several times, as I would be out walking and praying, the young lady's husband would drive up beside me and want to talk about all that was going on between his wife and my husband. He was very confused about what was going on, and he was searching for answers. I was not much help to him, but somehow we did seem to take comfort in talking to each other. He even told me one day he felt so bad I had to go through this. He told me I was a good woman, and it wasn't right for Dan to treat me like this; I had done nothing to deserve this. I actually came to like the young man. I felt so much compassion for him. I could see his heart was being crushed. I truly wished I could help him, but I just didn't have the answer. It made me sad he was not a Christian and he had to be involved in such a terrible experience as this with his wife and a preacher.

About this same time, Daniel decided to join the Army. He wrote on the enlistment form he was enlisting because he wanted to get away from his mother. He thought I was mean and too hard on him. He wanted to be out on his own. All of our children thought I was too hard on them because I had to fight their dad continually just to make them responsible and protect them from things that were harmful to them.

Of course, a few weeks in the Army convinced Daniel I had not been too hard on him. He had time to think about things and realized how much I loved him and I had done my best, in spite of everything, to help him be responsible and be able to be successful in life. Daniel called me one day from boot camp crying so hard I could barely understand him. He had been standing in line for a long time just to get to a pay phone so he could tell me he was sorry for all the trouble he had caused me. He said he now knew I only disciplined him because I loved him. He told me I should have been even tougher on him and not to let up on Mark and Sarah. It was the best thing I could do for them. Wow! That really thrilled my heart! I had done something right! From then on, Daniel and I had a much better relationship. We didn't always agree on everything, but he trusted me much more, and I could rely on him to be there when I needed him.

As things grew worse, I felt God calling me to pray and fast for Dan. I felt God wanted me to fast all food. I was to drink only water and some fruit juices for ten days. I had never gone that long without eating food before this time, but I knew God would give me the strength I needed to carry on my daily activities at school, church and home. He had always been so faithful to me. I wanted to do whatever it took to see Dan delivered from Satan's hold. I prayed, fasted and believed God would somehow turn Dan around and bring him back to the preacher, husband and father he used to be, before Satan pulled him completely away.

One night, about seven days into my fast, I was at home with our children when I got a phone call from Renee. She told me Dan was at a restaurant with some of our board members when a young man stood outside the plate glass window of the restaurant, in full view of everyone, and took a bat to our church van. He beat out the windows and was destroying the van. He was screaming at Dan and accusing him of trying to take his wife. The board members, who were present, were quite upset and were trying to settle things down. The police were called, and they hauled the young man off to jail as our board members and Dan continued to talk.

Soon, they moved their meeting to the church where they asked Dan if he wanted to pray. It was a night to behold! I, too, went to the church to meet and pray with them. As we prayed, the wife of the man in jail came storming into the church. She had blood running out of her nose and she was screaming for Dan. She was almost uncontrollable, but some of our men managed to hold her back as she tried to get into the room where Dan was praying with our prayer warriors. Soon the men convinced her to leave. She left, and we continued praying for quite some time.

We all became very much aware Satan was trying hard to destroy our church and school. He had done quite a number on Dan, and only God could help him out of this. We prayed and prayed! Dan was delivered of many demons that night. He left feeling and looking very different; however, there seemed to be something still not quite right. I think everyone knew it, but we went home praising God for the great progress Dan *had* made. We continued to pray God would keep working on him. I had tried so hard to believe in him and our marriage. I felt somewhat hopeful at this point but couldn't help but wonder why he couldn't be completely delivered from all the demons. *Why would he hold on to a demon, when he knew it was literally destroying his life?* This was such a puzzle to me! The fact Dan started acting and looking more like his old self made me so much more hopeful he would be able to be completely delivered.

However, during this time, God also began to show me Dan was very different from the man I used to know. He had taken on a whole new look. As I looked into his eyes, I didn't know who he was anymore. It was a very strange feeling. I didn't understand exactly what was going on until Dan finally told me. He had run into a demon, face to face, and he had invited the demon to come in. He said it gave him such a warm, good feeling. The demon came to him in the form of the young woman he was working with who also attended our church. After he invited the demon in, he became very attracted to this lady and that's why he hired her to work at our restaurant. He and this young woman had been spending quite a bit of time together. It was her husband who had just beaten up the church van in front of the restaurant and our board members.

As he talked, I knew I had to face all of this whether I liked it or not. I asked God to help me deal with it in the right way—in His way. I had to face the fact that Dan, at age 43, was having an affair with a 25-year-old married woman in our church. She just attended but had never made a commitment to God. We were supposed to be convincing her and her family to change their lives and follow Christ. How sad!

Dan thought I knew about the affair, so he started talking about it quite openly. I was very shocked but acted like it wasn't important, and I knew it all the time. I did know some things, but not all the facts he laid out that night.

After all this, the young woman came to church on Sunday with her husband. She was wearing sunglasses which she left on during the church service. Everyone knew who she was, and they felt the coldness that walked in with her. Dan told our Associate Pastor he could not preach with this woman staring at him and causing so much distraction. So, we went home and our Associate Pastor spoke to the congregation that morning.

The next week, our Associate Pastor asked to have a restraining order placed on her—to keep her away from the church and from Dan and me. She was not allowed to go within so many feet of our home, place of employment or anywhere else if she knew we were there. It was a very tense week. It was around March when we placed the restraining order. We ended up having to meet her and her husband in a judge's office. I assumed we were meeting in order for the judge to explain to all of us exactly what this order meant.

During the meeting, the young woman looked straight at me and threatened me—right in front of the judge! She was very vicious and said she would take care of me. She seemed to believe this was somehow all my fault. Also, at the meeting, the judge asked Dan if he had anything he wanted to say. Dan asked the young woman's husband to forgive him for the problems he had caused. He told the husband he wanted him to know he and his wife had only been having this "affair" since January of that year. Before that, it was just an emotional attachment. The attachment led to an affair before they realized what was happening. When Dan said the word "affair," the husband came out of his chair. He looked at his wife and said, "So, this *was* an affair?" All at once, he was not interested in anything else that was said. The meeting ended, and he flew off to his car. Later, we heard he drove straight to a lawyer's office and filed for divorce. As far as we know, the word never did get out around the church or the town that they had actually had an "affair." It was thought they had just become emotionally attached because of her counseling.

Dan took a leave from pastoring the church at that point, and we had to re-evaluate what we were doing. I continued to run the school, and it did quite well. We closed the restaurant and counted our losses. It didn't take long for Dan to realize he could never pastor this church again. He had lost all credibility. So, he told the church board, and they began to search for a new pastor. Dan and I began to make plans to move somewhere else where he would get a secular job. I hated to leave the school but felt I had no choice.

We did not tell our children exactly what had happened at this time. We only stated their dad had made some very bad decisions he was sorry for and we were going to move where he could find a secular job. The children seemed to take it very well. It was two years later when they found out their dad had actually had an affair. In fact, most everyone thought Dan had just made some bad choices with a relationship. They did not realize he had actually had an affair. We left it at that. There was no reason to hurt the name of the church any more than it had already been hurt.

Chapter 15

Going Downhill Together

Our next move was to Dallas, Texas. We knew jobs would be more abundant in that area, so off to Dallas we went. Dan worked at a sales job and was gone during the week; he came home only on the weekends. I was left at home all week without a car. I had no means of getting the children to school or anywhere else. We had to pay for rides everywhere we needed to go if we couldn't walk. We walked quite a bit, exploring to find out what was near us. I found a florist job very close to where we lived. I worked there temporarily. After a few months, I started taking a taxi cab to a cashier's job I found at a franchise lube shop.

As time went on, Dan stayed away from home a lot, but he managed to get home every weekend. Each weekend he'd come home and sell off our furniture one piece at a time until it was all gone. Soon, we were sitting on soda crates and barely having enough food to make it through each week. As time passed, I had to become more and more creative in making up our week's menu. I could see we weren't going to make it doing it this way much longer when our rent got behind. I wasn't sure what our next step would be.

Before long, Dan also realized we were not going to make it financially with him working on the road in sales and me at home with no car. He wanted us to find other employment. First, we tried caring for foster children who were on the verge of going to juvenile care. That did not work out well at all. Our children were teenagers, and they certainly did not need to be around problem teenagers all the time. They needed a more wholesome environment.

Next, Dan suggested I get a job at a place where they developed curriculum for Christian Schools and missionaries. I had previously wanted to work there, but we had lived too far away. The job didn't pay very much, but at least I could have steady work. I was so happy when he suggested we move closer to where I could find the work I enjoyed! In fact, we were all excited for the opportunity to be around Christian people again. I found I could enroll Mark and Sarah in the Christian School right on the campus where I would be working. Also, they could attend the school quite inexpensively, as a benefit for my being employed there. Things finally began to look up for the kids and me.

I thoroughly enjoyed my new career. I was placed in the International Office. It was our responsibility to answer questions, solve problems and send people back and forth overseas for training in how to operate a Christian School overseas. The people I worked with were pastors and missionaries and their wives. Many times, they traveled to Africa, India, South America, Russia, Mexico—all over the world. They were some of the most Christ-like people I have ever had the privilege of being with. I knew God had placed me in that particular office for a reason. I had asked to be placed in the Home Schooling Department, and the supervisor wanted me there and was excited I was coming. Somehow, all the placement instructions were changed at the last minute, and I was sent to the International Department. They hadn't even requested another person. They were as surprised as I was.

> *God guided those in charge of placement so I went to the exact place He wanted me to be.*

Once I got to know them better, they admitted they hadn't even asked for help, and they thought I was placed there to spy on them for some reason. They stayed very distant from me at first, until they realized I was placed there to work, not spy. I didn't understand it at first, but God knew exactly where He wanted me, and He guided those in charge of placement so I went to the exact place He wanted me to be. I worked in a wonderful atmosphere where devotions started our day and where it was easy to talk about the things of God. These people became like family to me. When I started going through deep waters, God showed me I could trust them. And He showed them how to help me.

Right after I started working for the curriculum developers, Dan was working at a home for juvenile teenagers, and I got a call from the County Sheriff's Department. They were asking to set up an appointment with Dan.

They needed to talk to him about a situation he had been contacted about earlier. Of course, I was unaware of their earlier contact. They needed to investigate and get a statement from Dan about what actually happened on a certain night while he was working at the home where teenage girls who had drug problems were staying. In a meeting with a social worker, one of the girls stated she had stayed up one night and spent the night with Dan while the other girls slept. She alleged she and Dan were involved in inappropriate behavior in the home that night. Dan was being questioned about his log for that night. He had logged in that the girl had gone to bed when the other girls went to bed. However, other girls remembered the girl in question had not gone to bed with them that evening. Dan was questioned on whether she actually went to bed or stayed up. He admitted she did, in fact, stay up after the others went to bed. He stated she was restless, so he let her watch TV with him in the main den area. The sheriff took a statement from Dan as they awaited the court case. During the wait, he was not allowed to work. In fact, he told me he had decided to quit. As far as I know, the case was dropped, and he never went back to the home again. He looked for employment elsewhere.

At the time this happened, I was shocked to think Dan was even accused of something so horrible. *Would he take advantage of these foster juveniles we were supposed to be helping to get straightened out?* I thought the girl was making this story up, and of course, Dan told me she was. I just couldn't understand why he didn't tell me he was being questioned by the County Sheriff's Department. *If he was innocent, why wouldn't he tell me the whole story and ask for my support during the whole episode? Why was he acting so secretive?* I never could understand this whole situation. Dan didn't want to talk about it, so it remained a mystery from then on. I just chose to believe he was innocent in order to be able to face him each day.

In the fall of 1992, Mark and Sarah both began their senior year of high school. The school on campus where I worked was a testing ground for the curriculum we were producing. The school taught from the "At-Your-Own Pace" (PACE) curriculum. Mark and Sarah both felt classroom teaching would be very beneficial for their senior year and prepare them better for college.

Therefore, I enrolled them in a Christian Academy just a couple of miles from where I worked. Several of their friends were going there, too. I was able to get a discount on tuition, so it worked out quite well.

After a few months of living in this area, Dan was also hired to work where I worked. I thought he enjoyed his work there. Soon, however, he began to get restless and started looking for something else. He found work first about 15 to 20 miles away. Then he changed jobs to work in an office even further south of us. He was hired to manage a temporary employment agency where they would pay their employees daily as they completed a day's work. Many people who were barely surviving came to find jobs there. As Dan would go to the office in the morning, many of the applicants would be sleeping on the cement around the employment agency. They were waiting for the doors to open so they could go in and get work for the day. It was sad to see people in such a condition but good that there was help—even just one day at a time.

Dan's father felt sorry for us and gave me a car to drive. We were thrilled! Dan finally had a good job, and I had a great job working with Christian people and Christian Schools. We had a great school for the kids, and now my own car to drive. What more could we want? About this same time, Daniel came home and wanted to live with us. We were quite happy to have him back. He got a job at the city Water Department making a little over minimum wage, but he was able to pay his own expenses. He even had a car that barely ran, but at least it was transportation for a while. Daniel could see things had gotten much worse while he was gone. I think he just hoped it would all work out.

One day, he told me his dad had asked him for the phone number of the young woman he had been caught having the affair with at our last pastorate. Daniel was very upset about it. I wondered why Dan would ask Daniel for his "old girlfriend's" phone number. *Did he think Daniel would give it to him and not tell me, his mother?* His actions were very disturbing to me. *Did he actually think my own son would betray me? Did he think Daniel would actually say nothing to me?* I asked Daniel if he gave it to him. Daniel said he didn't even have it. I found out later Dan did get the number from somewhere, but the young woman wouldn't even talk to him.

Before long, Dan started having trouble with his car, so he had to drive mine. The kids and I were left driving his car that smoked so badly they would hide on the floor when we went anywhere for fear they'd see someone they knew. Then Dan decided we should sell the older car since it was in need of repair, and we had no money to get it fixed. That meant the kids and I had to walk again! Soon, our water was turned off, and we couldn't pay our other bills. We were getting worse by the day. I couldn't understand why Dan wasn't bringing home the money he should be making. He finally sold the last of our furniture—our bed. He brought home a mattress he had picked up from somewhere, like a dump or mission maybe. It was dirty and in very bad shape. I covered it the best I could and tried to make do, but I knew we couldn't keep going like this. I just kept praying somehow Dan would wake up and see turning from God had not helped him at all. But he never did. It was as if he was completely blinded to the condition he was in. Sometimes, he laughed about it and even put a cartoon on our refrigerator door showing two kids going down a hill on their sled. The caption underneath it read: "Going downhill together."

I knew the end of all this had to be near. I knew unless Dan turned his life over to God very soon and received healing, he was going to allow Satan to totally destroy him. I didn't want to see that happen. I knew his new job was not at all good for him. He seemed to identify very closely to homeless people and those who had no purpose or future. That scared me! We were worse off financially, and he was getting worse off spiritually by the day. I continued to walk and pray. I knew something had to break soon.

By October, the situation with Dan had gotten so bad, I started asking God if He wanted me to stay with him. He was working late each night (so he said) and came home smelling like alcohol and acting very obnoxious. Most of the time, I pretended to be asleep so he wouldn't try to argue with me. His attitude toward me was, "You're lucky I'm here. So quit complaining about what I do." Any questions I asked were met with anger, ridicule and defensiveness. In his eyes, it seemed I could do nothing right. I wasn't allowed to voice my opinion very often and my talk about God only annoyed him. I had begun to feel like a prisoner when he was home, and I was a little afraid of him at times, so I tried not to upset him. As I walked and prayed daily, I began to let God prepare me for what was ahead.

Then one day as I was walking, I heard myself saying these words, "God, if it is Your will, take Dan away from me. I feel like I've gone as far as I can go. I've prayed and fasted all I can, and I see him only going farther and farther away from You and from me. You know what it's going to take to bring him back to You. Whatever that is, he's Yours. Take him and do whatever You have to do to bring him back to You."

Not long after that prayer, I began finding evidence Dan was again being unfaithful. He was so careless! It was as if he wanted me to know. The women he went out with were not church women, nor were they the type who would settle down and marry "until death do us part."

Finally, I confronted him and asked him to either quit going out on me or just quit coming home. I told him I thought he would have more respect for me than to expect me to live like this. That night, I told the kids for the first time their dad was seeing someone else, and I had told him I couldn't live like this any longer. I wasn't sure what he'd do. All three of them were shocked and asked me how long all of this had been going on and how could I have hidden it for so long? As we went to bed that night, none of us really considered Dan would leave. We felt he would

As I walked and prayed daily, I began to let God prepare me for what was ahead.

apologize and try to be more considerate. He gave no indication he wanted to end our marriage. The word "divorce" had never come up in our entire 27 years of marriage. I actually thought and hoped our conversation might have scared him a little. He covered up his real feelings quite well that evening.

Chapter 16

Desperation

The next day, October 23, 1992, Sarah called me at work and said she'd been in Study Hall when God spoke to her and told her to call me and give me a scripture to read:

Galatians 5:1 (KJV)
Stand fast therefore in the liberty wherewith Christ hath made us free, and be not entangled again with the yoke of bondage.

The NIV says it like this:

It is for freedom that Christ has set us free. Stand firm, then, and do not let yourself be burdened again by a yoke of slavery.

She read it to me and said, "Mom, I don't know what this means, but I know God told me to give it to you, so read it today." She had never done this before, so I told her I would, and I hung the phone up wondering what all this could mean. At 4:30 p.m., when I got off work and went home, I found out.

There was a note on the table from Dan saying, "Goodbye." He left each of us a note telling us how sorry he was, but he really needed to get away and think of himself now. He wanted us all to know we had done nothing wrong. He just wanted to make a change. He was tired of doing the "right thing." He wanted to do what he wanted to do now. We were all in shock! Did this mean he had only stayed with us because he felt he had to? We sat in the living room crying and reading our letters for a long time—unable to comprehend what was happening.

Daniel and Sarah were devastated! How could their dad leave them with only a letter? Mark had a football game that night and since it was out of town, we didn't go to see him play, and he wasn't home when we found the notes. As Daniel, Sarah and I sat there crying, Mark came bursting in the door exclaiming this was the best day of his entire life! He had made three touchdowns! As he started to go through each play, he realized all of us were crying. He stopped and asked, "What's wrong?" No one wanted to tell him. We finally told him his dad had written each of us a letter before he took all of his belongings and left. Mark became very visibly shaken. He started sobbing violently. We all felt so badly for him. At that point, we all focused on trying to comfort Mark and get him through this. All of us were in shock, but Mark seemed to be taking this the worst.

Soon, Sarah jumped up from the couch, started going through the house, moving everything around and saying, "I'm not going to let him do this to us. I am covering up all the places where he took things. We will not even notice he is gone! I am moving my things into Mom's room where Dad's stuff was. Mom will not be alone. I will be there." Somehow we got through the night by leaning on each other. I know God was there loving us and comforting us; otherwise, I don't know what we would have done.

Even though I had prayed earnestly and prepared myself emotionally and spiritually for whatever God wanted for my life, Dan's leaving devastated me. Somehow, I just believed God would reach his heart and turn him around. I found it so hard to believe he could not only have betrayed me, his best friend for 33 years, but that anyone who loved God the way Dan had could ever make such a turnaround and go against God like this. He was blatantly turning his back on all he knew to be good and right. He even told me he was tired of doing the right thing. How many times had I heard him preach about this very thing and warn others that Satan was tricky, and he was a thief and a liar. He warned that Satan would gradually steal your life and leave you alone, empty and without the joy of the Lord that had been your source of strength and the reason to live.

One sermon he had preached reminded me exactly of what had happened to him. He brought someone up front and tied string around his arms so he was bound and restricted from moving. With one, two or even three strings, he could break the string and free his arms. But the more strings he tied around him, the harder it was to break. He compared the string to Satan's hold on our lives. The more we allow him to bind us up with sin, wrongdoings, habits, wrong thoughts or actions, the harder it is to break away and get free again. If we allow sin to continue to have a hold on us, it will gradually (one string at a time) bind us up until we cannot break away—just as the person he had tied up with the string could not break away. He explained we then have to call on God with all our heart, and we even need to ask for other Christians to pray and call upon the power of God, too. He alone can deliver us from the hold Satan has on our lives. He stressed how we should always be open to God's correction and keep our hearts soft and our conscience clear toward God—to never allow several strings to get tied around us. Then, we'll never become so hardened we can't break those strings and in the process lose that joy, peace and love only God can put in our hearts.

That sermon continues to run through my mind today as I wonder why Dan wouldn't have listened to that advice himself. He did exactly what he'd warned others not to do. Look at all the pain and unhappiness he was bringing to himself, as well as his wife, children, friends and family.

The "Goodbye letters" he left devastated all of us. We cried all night. It was like a morgue in our home for several weeks. None of us could understand how our family could have come to this. Sarah said it perfectly when she said, "I always thought we had the perfect family, and I was so happy. How could this happen?" At one time, I thought that, too. I thought there was no other family, anywhere, as happy as we were. I felt God had truly blessed us abundantly, above and beyond! I used to look at other people with problems and feel so sad for them because they didn't know the happiness we felt. I never dreamed this would ever happen to us!

I remember hurting so badly I would break out crying at any time and any place. It just happened, and I seemed to have no control over the tears. Some nights, I would lie in bed crying and wondering if this pain would ever go away. I had heard of some people dying from a broken heart and wondered if I would live through this. I actually had such pain in my heart area I wondered if my heart was actually breaking in two. The only two things that kept me going were my faith in God to "work all things for my good" because I loved Him and trusted Him, and secondly, my three children. I knew my three children were leaning very hard on me to show them how to get through this. I knew I could never let them down.

I took a course on "Grieving," and I went to a Christian Counseling Center for help and encouragement. My children went, too. Both places helped us quite a bit. I know I must have been a burden to all my friends and family during that time; however, I was hurting so badly, I couldn't help it. I just had to talk and talk and keep talking to work through all the grief and pain. At one point, I noticed God was putting me on their hearts at different times and different days. One would call one day and another would call the next. It was as if someone was orchestrating my phone calls so I talked to a different friend each evening after work. I realized I was talking to a friend every evening, going through all my pain, over and over again, trying to figure it all out but to a different person each evening. I would have worn one person completely out! Only God knew how to plan all those calls. I was so thankful my friends were all there for me.

> "Go to God with all your needs, but never get caught up in self-pity. It will destroy you!"

That first year was extremely hard to get through. I couldn't even taste food when I ate it, and I lost about twenty pounds. It took a whole year before I got my appetite back. The intense pain lasted about that long, and then the pain was just off and on. It would come over me like ocean waves. Some days, I'd do okay; other days, I'd be so overwhelmed again with pain I would feel like I was back to zero again—starting all over.

But I had one thought constantly going through my head. It was something Grandma had told me: "If you ever start feeling sorry for yourself, remember that self-pity is straight from the devil. Don't ever let him trick you into that. Go to God with all your needs, but never get caught up in self-pity. It will destroy you!" I believe that advice saved me much heartache. It brought me through this overwhelming experience knowing God really loved me and only wanted the best for me. I thanked Him continually for all He was doing in my life rather than feeling sorry for myself.

Without God's love during that time, I could never have made it. My children told me later they worried about me and were afraid they'd lose me, too. They took turns staying home with me or they took me with them wherever they went. One day, it occurred to me I was hanging around with teenagers all the time. They all seemed to want me, so I guess it was okay. My children and I grew extremely close during this time, and we all leaned heavily on God to carry us through.

I was not only devastated emotionally but financially. I had no way of paying the bills. It was in the middle of the school year, and Mark and Sarah were in their senior year at the Academy, which now I couldn't pay for. I lived in a home which I couldn't pay for. I had no car, no furniture, very few clothes, and I made $5.50 an hour. When I looked at my budget, it was perfectly clear to me my expenses were triple my income. At first I panicked, until God spoke to me very clearly through the Scriptures and said, *"I will be your husband."* Even though I would read about how God was a husband to the widow, I knew the words were also meant for me. Those words jumped off the page at me, and I felt God was speaking them to me.

Isaiah 54:4–6 (NIV)
"Do not be afraid; you will not be put to shame. Do not fear disgrace; you will not be humiliated. You will forget the shame of your youth and remember no more the reproach of your widowhood. For your Maker is your husband—the Lord Almighty is his name—the Holy One of Israel is your Redeemer; he is called the God of all the earth. The Lord will call you back as if you were a wife deserted and distressed in spirit—a wife who married young, only to be rejected," says your God.

Then one morning, seven weeks after Dan left, as I took my morning shower, God spoke to me in a very loving, clear, audible, God-like voice, and said, ***"I will provide for you! Just as I provided the sacrifice for Abraham on the mountain, I will provide for you."*** God knew I needed confirmation of His love and that He would watch over me, and He let me know He was there, right by my side. I always put my tithe in church every Sunday morning and was generous to other people as I trusted God to take care of me. From that day to this, He truly has provided for me—He never has failed to provide for my every need.

From the time Dan left, so many miracles took place in our lives I started logging them on my calendar. I wrote down our needs and the day I asked God for help, and then I'd write on the date how God answered prayer and provided for us.

One thing became clear to me very quickly: If I needed it, God provided it! Even years after these experiences, it is still heavily impressed on my heart that if I need it, God will provide it for me, and if He doesn't, it is because I really don't need it. I have learned time and time again: *"this same God who takes care of me will supply all your needs from his glorious riches, which have been given to us in Christ Jesus"* (Philippians 4:19, NLT). Sometimes He even provides some of our wants. The following scripture in His Word was reality to me then and still is to me now.

Psalm 84:11 (NLT)
For the Lord God is our sun and our shield. He gives us grace and glory. The Lord will withhold no good thing from those who do what is right.

Though those days were some of the toughest I ever walked through, they were also the days I felt God's Presence the most—more than any other days of my life up until then. He literally "provided" for me. When I had a need, I laid it before Him, and He truly took care of it. Most of the first year, I watched in amazement at all He was doing.

From the time Dan left, I felt such intense pain and brokenness because he had betrayed me. The rejection was very painful for years to come. In the middle of all this pain, I had to lean solely on God for not only food and provisions, but for love and courage to go on, for wisdom in counseling the kids and for my every need. My faith in God grew more each day as I lived through one miracle after another. Soon, I was totally convinced He really did care, and He really was my *Provider*—*in every way!*

One of the first things God helped me with was a car. Daniel had his car, but it was ready for the dump. It barely got him where he needed to go, and I was afraid to even drive it. Even after Daniel traded his car in for another one, he was gone to another town all day to work, and I had no way to get to work or get the kids to school other than walk. Dan left with our only vehicle, so we were left walking again. This time, God had other plans for us. On October 26, the very day I told my employer my husband had left me and my children, my boss, Mr. Grant, wrote me a letter telling me he wanted to be obedient to God and help me with transportation. He gave me his second car for as long as I needed it. He would even pay the insurance. I just had to put gas in it and drive it. Mr. Grant felt God had blessed him with a second car, and God wanted him to bless me.

I had to lean solely on God for not only food and provisions, but for love and courage to go on, for wisdom in counseling the kids and for my every need.

I was so glad he followed God's leading! Having a car was such a help in getting to work and getting the kids to school, as well as just going to the store, church, etc. I guess God knew all along what plans He had for me. Mrs. Grant agreed to it, too, even though it meant she didn't have a car of her own; they would have to share a car. I know that was an inconvenience for them, but I thanked God so much for people like the Grants who were willing to obey God and give up their own convenience to help me. God knew to place me near people like the Grants who had a real heart for Him and people. I pray I will always be available to bless others as the Grants blessed me.

When I figured out my budget, it looked impossible and useless to even try to decide when to pay what. So for the first time in my life, I put aside "my budget" and just let God bring the money as the need arose. The house payment was the first big hurdle I had to get over, so I made a phone call just to see if there was any possible way of deferring or paying a partial amount. I wasn't really sure what I hoped to accomplish by the call, but I just felt by calling I *might* work something out.

When the company representative answered and we started talking, she told me I didn't owe the usual amount this month. It had been reduced to $129.00 due to some extra money in the account. I nearly cried. I was so happy! I didn't even try to check out why the money was there. I knew somehow God knew it needed to be there just at the right time. That meant I had my house payment paid for another month. I was so thankful! Then Daniel agreed to help pay part of the house payment. He wasn't making much yet, but at least he could help with that for a while even though it would take most of what he had. It left very little for him once he paid it.

The next challenge was the groceries. I was concerned especially for the kids. I wasn't sure just what to buy or not to buy, so I turned it all over to God again. Friday, October 30, one week after Dan left, I went to get into my "new" car and found the back seat completely filled with groceries. I was absolutely amazed! I wondered who had put them there! I found out the people in my office had decided God wanted them to buy my groceries *every week!* They asked me to make a list of what we liked and needed, and they would take care of buying groceries for me. What a blessing these people were! *They* were so blessed by helping *me*, joy just burst out all over *them!* They not only bought what I needed, they bought above and beyond anything I could have asked for. They bought the "best" of everything. My children commented we had better food then than we'd had before. These wonderful friends truly gave from hearts of love and as if they were doing it for God. I felt so much love and was so blessed to be working with "God's people." They continued buying groceries for us until the middle of December.

As my bills came due each month, I told no one. I just trusted God. After all, He had said *He* would be *my Husband,* and He had promised to provide. I received my utility bills month after month, and I laid them out before Him in prayer. A few days later, the money would come, either through the mail, from someone at my church, or I would find an envelope on my desk marked: "I felt like God told me to give you this." This happened week after week and month after month. Every need was supplied just as I needed it. I received money from people I had not seen or talked to in months.

There were a few incidents when I had special needs I also turned over to God, and He came through. One day in December, Sarah was having severe cramps and was barely able to go to school. She didn't know if she could make it through the day. As I left for work, she was crying and asked if I could please buy some Ibuprofen. It had been the only thing that seemed to give her relief, previously. I felt terrible about her pain but didn't have the money to buy any. I said, "Sarah, I know you need Ibuprofen, but it's so expensive. I just can't buy anything right now. You will have to take the aspirin we have and make it do for now." I then left for work which was five minutes from the house. I got out of the car, walked into the building and ran into a friend who had a bottle of Ibuprofen in her hand! She said, "I just thought maybe you could use this." I started crying. Again, I knew God really was taking care of us. No one else even knew how badly I felt about not having the money to buy that pain reliever for Sarah. How wonderful God cared so much! Even little things like our needing Ibuprofen mattered to Him. And I was so grateful again for friends like Lori who listened to His voice and obeyed His prompting.

During this time, I lost my appetite, and I was losing weight pretty quickly. Within a few months, my uniform for work was about two sizes too big. The uniforms were specially ordered and very expensive. I wasn't sure what to do. My uniform was looking way too big for me, and I couldn't hide that it was about to fall off of me. Of course, this was January, and by then I knew I just needed to tell God my needs. In just a few days, a lady in the office next to us asked if we knew of anyone who could use an almost new uniform she had outgrown. She gave it to me, and I finally had a great looking uniform to wear that fit perfectly! Of course it did! God did above and beyond anything I imagined.

We were getting ready for work and school one day. Everything was very hectic, and Mark and Sarah's friend who was going to pick them up for school, was running very late. Sarah went outside to move the car so I could take her and Mark to school. She backed it up and ran into his car just as he was pulling in to pick them up. Even though she had her driver's license, it was a real tragedy because the Grants didn't have insurance on anyone under the age of 25. I felt terrible! We all did! The car was drivable, but a light was busted, and there was a dent in the back bumper. I took it in for an estimate and it came to $189.95. In 1992, that was a lot more money than it seems now—especially to me. Of course, I had no money, and I sure didn't want the Grants to pay to fix a car my daughter wrecked. Again, I took it to God in prayer. I asked Him to please help and send me a check for the repairs on the car. It wasn't right that the Grants should have to pay for the repairs. Also, I said, "God, could You make it for the exact amount to repair the car so I'll know what it's for?" I was receiving so many checks I wanted to really be sure God was saying this check was for car repairs.

I went to church on Sunday morning, November 22, and sang in the choir. During the offering, my friend's husband, Jim, who was an usher, came up to me in the choir loft and handed me a check—for exactly the amount of what I needed to repair the car! After church, I met Jim and Cathy to thank them for the money. I told them I knew God had led them to give it to me because it was exactly the amount I needed to repair my car, and I mentioned the amount. Jim looked at Cathy and said, "Why did you write the check for that amount?" They had talked about giving me a totally different amount earlier. She said, "I don't know. As I wrote it, I just felt like that was the amount we were to give her, so I did." We all cried, and I thanked God for obedient people who listen and obey when God speaks. Jim and Cathy cried because they felt so blessed God had used them in such a real, tangible way and because they had listened and obeyed when He spoke. Another time, they brought me a brand new washing machine when they found out I was having to go to the laundromat. (I had given my washing machine to someone in exchange for them taking my children to school.)

On another occasion in May, I had asked God to help me with the expenses for Mark and Sarah's high school graduation. There were so many things they wanted like senior pictures, new outfits, caps and gowns and senior trip expenses. I had no money to pay for any of them. On May 14, before graduation, I was in a restaurant with Cathy, and as we walked through the line, she pulled a check for $538.00 out of her purse and said, "Jim and I wanted to give you some money to help out with your expenses. We had a really good month and felt we should share with you." I was in shock; I never dreamed I would ever receive that much help—and at a fast food restaurant! I knew exactly what it was for. I thanked God so much for providing my children with the things they wanted to make their high school graduation a really happy occasion. God again was showing Himself to be my *Husband* and my *Provider* even in things that weren't necessities. He continually provided above and beyond all we could have hoped for. Mark and Sarah graduated with all their desires met. God truly was their Father, and He cared far more than any earthly father ever could.

There was an incident that happened several months after God had been providing for us that shows just how confident my children and I had become of God's provision. Our electric bill was due, and I hadn't received the money to pay it. This was the first time I had a bill due and God hadn't given me the money to pay it. It was so puzzling to me! I was sitting on the couch crying. *What could have happened? Where was the money for the electric bill? Had I missed it somewhere?* I knew God wouldn't fail me, but where was the money? I had never had to pay a bill late from the time Dan walked out the door.

As I was sitting on the couch, my children came home. They asked me what was wrong. I told them I hadn't gotten any money to pay the electric bill, and it was going to be late if I didn't pay it now. Daniel said, "Mom, did you find that envelope I put in your bedroom the other day? It came in the mail, but you weren't here, so I put it in your room. Don't you remember me telling you?" As I stood up to go to my bedroom, new hope arose in all our hearts. I walked into my bedroom, picked up the envelope, held it up in the air and said, "What do you think will be in this envelope?" The kids all said at once, "The money for the electric bill!" I opened the envelope to find a check for the exact amount of our electric bill. Again, God had not failed us. We just had to figure out where His check was. I had missed it. He was on time—just as He always was.

Time and time again, God provided for all of our needs. I could never record all of the things He supplied—both physically and emotionally. Many times, I felt as though He was walking right by my side. I felt His love so strongly! God *was* my *Husband*, and He provided for me far better than any human man ever could. It was an experience that changed me forever! I learned just how much He really loves me and that He truly is my *Provider.* Even now, when I think about things I want or think I need, I know He will provide for all of my needs as I walk close to Him and do His will. He knows what's best for me, and I trust Him completely. He will never leave me to live this life alone; He wants to walk right beside me to lead me and guide my every step, my every decision. How could I not continue to trust and follow Him when He's proven His love for me over and over again?

Chapter 17

Trauma Continues

In the spring of 1993, we found out from Dan's sister he and his new girlfriend were expecting a baby! Our divorce had not even gone through yet, but I was so glad I had filed the papers. His baby was to be born in October. What a shock that was to all of us! He had made it clear to me he wanted no more children—*ever.* He said he was finished with that stage of his life. He hated having little children around, making messes and leaving toys in the driveway. He even made that statement from the pulpit one day. He was so done with little children he insisted I have surgery so we would not have any more babies. So I did.

By then, Dan had moved to Georgia and then on to Florida. At that time, he and his new girlfriend were living with his sister and her family in Florida. His new girlfriend already had three children of her own—all under seven years of age! She was twenty years old and had never been married. Now he had a family of five to support and another baby on the way.

He came here for a visit and wanted to meet with me. He said God had called him to take care of this new family; they needed him. He felt he was finished raising our three children now that they were grown.

As Dan talked, I couldn't help but think how far down he had fallen spiritually. In such a short time, he had forgotten what the Bible said about marriage and adultery. I felt like I was talking to a person who knew nothing about the Bible. He seemed to have no sign of guilt or conviction that he was doing wrong. *Had he seared his conscience that much? Or maybe that was a demon talking. Had Satan stolen his memory? What happened to the preacher who knew the Bible inside and out?* It was so puzzling to me.

The 1993 school year had been extremely difficult for all of us, but for Mark it was almost an impossible task. The principal told us Mark was distracted by his dad's letter. Everyone was quite concerned over his state of mind. I took him to counseling at a Christian Counseling Center. After several months, his counselor told me that trying to get through to Mark was like trying to break through a brick wall. He couldn't get anywhere. He told me Mark was like a stick of dynamite ready to blow at any moment. I was very concerned but had no other choice. All I could do was pray and wait to see what would happen to him. Mark couldn't concentrate on school work or anything else. The school principal and I became good friends during this time. He and his assistant called me many times trying to figure out how to get through to Mark and how to help him finish his schooling so he could graduate. I was so glad the principal continued to work with him all year as he tried to get through the shock of his father's leaving.

Finally, it was the last two weeks of school for the year. The principal called me to say he was advising Mark to stay home from the Senior Trip because he had managed to finish all of his requirements except for one subject. To complete that subject, there was a research paper due, and Mark was just now ready to start on it. This paper took his best students a minimum of two months to complete. He was just praying Mark could come up with some type of research paper in two weeks that would get a passing grade. Then he could take the final test and be able to graduate. The principal told me he had his doubts Mark could pull himself together enough to write the required paper, but he really wanted him to try.

Mark agreed to stay home from the Senior Trip and work on the research paper. At that point in his life, he didn't really care about anything—even a Senior Trip. When I saw the name of the research paper, my spirit really fell: "The Great Wall of China." I left him alone, just praying he could concentrate enough to write a passing paper in two weeks. Soon, I noticed he seemed to be enjoying the research he was doing and occasionally he would come tell me something new he had just learned. I wondered how anybody could love learning about The Great Wall of China so much; however, that subject seemed to be very interesting to Mark, and it took his mind off of everything else. He worked hard for those two weeks and seemed to love what he was doing. It was good to see him excited about something and doing so well for a change—even if it was over The Great Wall of China.

On the day of graduation, Mark turned in his research paper. The teacher accepted the paper and began grading it. He was so shocked he couldn't believe his eyes. Mark's research paper was one of the best he had ever read. He told me Mark had tremendous potential. He had not recognized it all year because of his state of mind. The paper was an absolute "A," and he was going to give Mark the final semester test to see if he could graduate that evening. He took the test and did very well. At 5:00 p.m., the principal called me to say, "Mark is going to graduate tonight!" He was so thrilled, and so was I! What a year it had been, but finally, Mark was making progress.

He loved history, and once he got his mind on The Great Wall of China for two weeks, he started thinking again and began to come out of his "stupor." I thank God for The Great Wall of China. I began to realize what a history buff Mark was! I knew he liked history, but for him to get that involved in it and do so well on the research paper was something only God could have planned. Mark and Sarah graduated in May of 1993. We had finally gotten over *a great big hurdle*.

Soon after graduation, we moved to Euless, Texas, into a townhouse. My parents decided to buy a townhouse so my brother, John, and I could share it. John's wife had left him, and he came to Texas to get away from all of the conflict going on where he had been living. He went house hunting and found the townhouse. This meant we would have a much better place to live. It was also much closer to our church. Having John around was a huge answer to prayer. I had asked God to please send someone who could help me fix things around the house and on the car. God sent John just when I needed him. Daniel had moved out during this time and was living in a garage apartment that belonged to some of our friends. It put him closer to his job. The townhouse arrangement worked out quite well for all of us until that December, when my brother met a young lady, fell in love and decided to move out into his own place. From then on, all expenses were mine. I thought finances might get a little tougher, but soon I was hired on staff at my church. Between that check and God's provision, we made it just fine. When I did fall short, God always made up the difference. I worked hard during the daytime, and I began to take night classes. My aptitude tests all said I should do accounting, so that's what I worked on.

After fourteen months of working at my church, I applied for a payroll position at a medical company nearby. The owner attended my church. He had hired several people from our church to work there. I decided to make the change. I was so excited when I was called in for an interview and offered the job. I even knew the people who would be training me. God was so good to me! The owner was such a godsend to my family. He hired me, my daughter *and* my son, Mark. He will never know what a blessing he was to my family. To this day, almost twenty years later, I send him a Christmas card each year just to thank him for all he did to help us. God worked miracles through that owner—just for me. I was so glad he was there and gave me that opportunity to get into accounting. I worked at the medical supply company until they were bought out by another company who transferred their payroll to Florida. I learned so much working there, enough to get another very good paying payroll job. I finally had experience and knowledge enough to make a living doing accounting. As I look back, I can see God ordering my steps one step at a time. How exciting to walk with God and know He will always provide more than enough as He teaches me how to provide for myself!

> *When I did fall short, God always made up the difference.*

In 1994, Dan came back to Texas for a visit. He stayed with Daniel but asked me to meet him at a restaurant so we could talk. By this time, his baby boy was a few months old. I met him and found he wanted to tell me God had spoken to him in church on Sunday morning. He said God told him to read Malachi 2:13–14 which talks about God not accepting your gifts or listening to your prayers because you are treating the wife of your youth treacherously. He told me after reading that scripture, he knew he had to come back to Texas and talk to me and ask my forgiveness for leaving me and hurting me like he had. I thought, up to that time, I had forgiven him. When he asked for forgiveness, he seemed to think all he had to do was say, "Forgive me," and it was all settled. He would then be free to go back home, to his girlfriend and his new family, and he would have God's blessings. At first, I was confused. Then I heard myself saying, "You have no earthly idea what you've done! Do you know the pain you've caused me and your children? Do you think you can make everything right by coming down here and just asking for my forgiveness? You're not sorry. You still aren't willing to do anything to make things right."

As I sat there raging, I realized I had not completely forgiven Dan. I was devastated! I had cried out to God over and over again about Dan, and I thought I had totally forgiven him. However, at that point, I knew for sure I hadn't. All I could think of was the same old stuff. *After 27 years of marriage, three children, 33 years of friendship and sharing my heart and life with this man, how could he just leave me a note on the kitchen table saying he didn't love me anymore, but could we continue to be friends? Didn't I deserve more than that? How could he possibly do this to me? And then getting this girl pregnant when he was still married to me! Having a child with another woman! That was unbelievable! How can I possibly forgive him for that?* As my mind rehearsed all of my pain again, I felt such a conviction inside me this was not right. All I could think of was, *"God, he needs to suffer for what he's done. How can I forgive him?"*

After that talk at the restaurant, I went home knowing quite well my heart was still very angry. I knelt beside my bed and cried, "God, help me! I don't know how to forgive him. I know You've told me in the Bible I have to forgive, but I don't know how!" I started to realize I had been making a very bad mistake. I had continued to rehearse my pain over and over again. I would never be able to forgive my ex-husband if I couldn't quit going over and over all that hurt, but how could I quit? Finally, I cried out again, "God, help me! I can't do this on my own; I don't know how to forgive him. Show me how to forgive him. I want to serve You, but I can't do it with all of this unforgiveness in my heart. Please, please, help me!" I was so desperate to know the answer.

As I sobbed and cried out from the depths of my heart, I heard God's voice speaking to me very clearly. *"My daughter, you will know how much you've forgiven him by your feelings toward his baby."* I sat up in shock. "God, You know I hate that baby! I've prayed for that baby to die. I've even asked for that baby to bring him the kind of pain he's given me. How can You ask me to love the one thing that hurts me the most?" No matter how much I argued, God continued to tell me to love that baby if I truly wanted to forgive my ex-husband. Finally, I surrendered my will to God's will. I said, "Okay God, if that's what You want me to do, I'll do my best. I can't stand to live without Your blessings on my life. I truly do love You, and I know You only want what's best for me." I went to sleep believing God would show me how to do what He was asking me to do.

Daily, I began to pray for that baby! At first, it didn't seem natural, and I didn't feel like I meant it, but soon it became easier and easier. I asked God to help me learn to love that baby as my own. Day by day I prayed blessings on the baby. I prayed he'd be a blessing to his parents, and he'd grow to be God's instrument and lead others to Christ. I asked God to give him a life of true joy and that he'd always follow in Christ's ways. I prayed for his happiness. The more I prayed for him, the more I began to care about him. Then one day I realized, even though I'd never seen him, I felt like I loved that little boy. What a change! God had truly changed my heart.

Then one day, my chance came to prove I had truly forgiven. Dan called and asked to come for a visit. He wanted to see the kids and me. I agreed he could come to see us. Then the clincher came: "Can I bring Thomas, my son?" My heart stood still as I mustered up the courage to answer: "Of course, you can bring Thomas." As soon as I hung up the phone, I felt numb. *Will I really love this baby when I see him? Will I pass the test? Have I really forgiven Dan this time?* "God, help me to truly forgive!"

As the time drew near, I prayed more and more for Thomas. Finally, I knew beyond a shadow of a doubt I loved him. The day he came in the door of my home, I felt drawn to him. He was so sweet and so cute, and he looked a lot like Daniel. What really surprised me was how he immediately took to me. He wanted to be with me the whole time he was there. I even had to lie down beside him so he'd go to sleep. Dan made the comment: "I don't understand this. Thomas never takes to strangers like this." The baby actually cried when he had to leave me. We had developed such a bond, my heart felt empty to see him go. I sat back in such relief! "God, I truly do love that little guy." God seemed to say back to me, *"And now you know you truly have forgiven Dan."* I was so excited; I could hardly stand it. My heart felt so light, and I had a peace like I'd never experienced before. Forgiving felt so good!

Still, many years later, Satan occasionally tries to tempt me to rehearse all that pain and heartache again, but I refuse to do it. It's then I'm reminded to pray for Thomas. Quickly, the bad thoughts go away. God's peace and joy once more flow through my heart. He truly has taught me how to forgive. Why not? He's the Master Forgiver! Hanging on an old rugged cross, He cried out, "Father, forgive them for they know not what they do" (Luke 23:34). I am so glad I listened to Him and learned to truly forgive. It has made all the difference in my life. I have been able to go on to find true joy and happiness without bitterness. Bitterness was like a poison to me. I was drinking the poison and hoping it would kill Dan instead of me. After I learned to forgive Dan, I was ready to go on with life and put all my past pain and hurt behind me. Life again began to be purposeful and exciting. I could truly laugh and enjoy all the wonderful things God had done for me.

In February 1995, Daniel was married and later that year, my first grandson was born. What an exciting time! It was hard for me to believe I was actually a grandma. Now I had two more family members to pray for. I was determined this new child would know God's love and learn to serve Him with all his heart. I would pray for him continually. Then, in February of 1996, my daughter was married. My family was growing very fast. Next, Mark announced his wedding plans for that same summer. Excitement was everywhere! Wedding plans and baby talk were all around me. It was a great time for me. I was so excited for my children and my new grandson who was quickly becoming the new love of my life.

One day, while I was enjoying my job and enjoying all of God's wonderful blessings, I received a call from a young lady in Louisiana. As she described herself, I began to remember who she was. She was the dark-eyed girl who was standing in our driveway the day we left our church in Louisiana to move to

Arkansas. She was in her mid-twenties now and said she had wanted to talk to me for some time but hadn't known how to find me. She said she had hated me for many years and wanted me to know she had been in counseling, and she now realized she had no reason to hate me. She said she was very sure now she had been lied to 13 years ago.

As I listened to this young lady, I began to feel shock come over my entire body. She told me she had come to our house to babysit because she had a big crush on my oldest son. However, while she was there, Dan had taken her into our back bedroom and molested her. He told her there was no reason for her to try to tell me. I already knew what he was doing, and we were in the process of getting a divorce. She said Dan had also taken her back in the woods at our church camp and again molested her in our car. I asked her questions about several things going on at that time: what type of car, things about our bedroom, etc. She remembered most of it very clearly. She said she had blocked it out of her memory for years. Recently, she had been having problems and her husband had convinced her to see a counselor. He had talked to her and helped her to remember the source of all her confusion and anger for the past 13 years. The girl's aunt and uncle were on our church board at the time we pastored there; I knew them very well. She told me I could talk to them any time I wanted to. The young lady had come to church with her grandmother. Her parents did not attend our church.

I soon talked to the girl's aunt and found she had actually gone to the counselor herself, just to be sure she understood what had happened to her niece. The aunt confirmed to me there was no doubt the girl was telling the truth. I told her it was very hard for me to believe all of this. The aunt said, "I can promise you that you can believe it. It's all very true."

I asked why no one was told about all this at the time. Did the girl tell anyone? I learned she told her grandmother who was a member of our church. The grandmother had called Dan before church one Sunday evening before church services. She asked to have a meeting with him after church that Sunday night. This just happened to be the same night Dan became very confused as he was preaching and had the nervous collapse in the pulpit. The grandmother never could get to him again. She also stated she didn't think anyone in the church would have believed her if she had just gone to the board. The girl's aunt was very sorry to say the grandmother was probably right. They were all so taken in by Dan's charismatic personality, no one would have believed the grandmother or the girl over Dan. As I hung up the phone, I felt very weak, and my mind was just not able to comprehend what I had heard. It took a very long time before this could really sink into my head.

As I cried and prayed about what I had just learned, I began to feel my whole adult life as a pastor's wife had been wasted. With all my heart, I had supported and stood behind a man who preached the Word of God. I had worked so hard to win people to Christ and get them into our churches throughout those 25 years. Now I find this man I had believed in as a man of God had destroyed the lives of how many people? *Was this girl just one of many he had destroyed along the way? What about those he had seen saved at the altars and were now leaving the church because they found out he himself wasn't serving Christ anymore?* I cried out to God with a broken heart. I felt like my heart would literally break in two as I thought about all the people who might be lost because we had pastored their church. And then I thought, *"People thought I knew what Dan was doing. So everything I've done was all in vain, too!"*

> *I was drinking the poison and hoping it would kill Dan instead of me.*

All at once, I heard this voice speaking to me, "Who did you do all of this for?" As I looked up, I thought about what that question meant. Why had I stayed with Dan for so many years and worked so hard to keep him preaching and pastoring? I knew the answer without a doubt. I answered, "I did it for You, Lord." I truly had done it because I wanted to see people saved and serving God. I wanted their lives to be meaningful, and I wanted them to know the great love of God I had known for so many years. Then I heard God speak again. He said, "If you did it for Me, it was not done in vain." All at once, my heart began to beat happily again. My life's work had not been in vain! God would use my life to help those I'd been in contact with. He would allow my life to be a testimony because I was doing it for Him, not for any other reason. Dan would have to answer for his own wrongdoings. I, however, was doing my very best to bring people into God's Kingdom. I honestly had no idea Dan was hurting people like this young girl. I didn't have to answer for him. God made it very clear to me that day He knew my heart. He had used me in ways I may never know, all for His Kingdom and His Glory. That day ended up being a wonderful day. God turned everything around and gave me a new excitement to continue serving Him.

1 Samuel 16:7 (NKJV)
But the Lord said to Samuel, "Do not look at his appearance or at his physical stature, because I have refused him. For the Lord does not see as man sees; for man looks at the outward appearance, but the Lord looks at the heart."

1 Corinthians 15:58 (NKJV)
Therefore, my loved brethren, be steadfast, immovable, always abounding in the work of the Lord, knowing that your labor is not in vain in the Lord.

These scriptures began to take on new meaning for me. Only God could turn my darkness to dawn. He put a new, stronger desire in my heart to serve Him as I went into a brand new phase of my life! I was excited to say the least.

Chapter 18

Venturing Out Cautiously

Even with all the excitement of weddings and a new grandson, early in 1996, I felt God was telling me to do something very strange. I felt very strongly He wanted me to join a Christian singles group called Equally Yoked. This was **totally** out of character for me. I was still somewhat shy and very conservative in my thinking. I had to get to know someone very well before I would ever go out with them. I didn't know how this would ever work out for me. I had not dated at all since Dan left in 1992, so this was a little scary to me. This meant I hadn't actually been on a date since 1965! It just seemed I could not get away from this feeling there was someone at Equally Yoked God wanted me to meet. I kept hearing about this group everywhere I went—on the radio, at church, around friends and even my family started telling me I needed to go there. I kept praying about whether this was God wanting me to go or just everybody else.

Finally, in April of 1996, I prayed, "Okay God, if You are telling me to go to Equally Yoked, please send me the money to join this group. You know it costs more money than I have." Within days, my mother called and asked me how much it cost to join Equally Yoked. Soon, I received the money in the mail. She told me she just felt like I was supposed to join. I held onto the money for a short while just thinking about whether I was really ready to meet someone, date, etc. I thought, *"I just can't do this right now. God, are You sure I'm ready for this?"* I finally loaned the money to my son. Then, in a month, when he paid me back, I decided I had to join.

In May 1996, I went in for an interview and felt like this was right. I made an appointment to record a video and join the club. As I joined, I felt very strongly God had a very special someone He wanted me to meet. I told God this dating thing was not for me, but if He really had someone He wanted me to meet, to please help me know who he was right away so I wouldn't have to date around to find him. I went in to look at the pictures of all the members. They were listed chronologically from the date each member had joined. Starting from the beginning, I looked through the entire membership. As I neared the end, I thought, *"What is going on here? I have absolutely no pull toward any of these men. I don't feel that any of these men are right for me."* Then, I turned the last page, and I saw the very last picture. As I looked at the picture, something inside me clicked. I thought, *"There he is."* I had the most peaceful assurance this was the man God wanted me to meet. I decided to look at his video to see what he was like. As he spoke about wanting God's will most in his life and about what was most important to him, I knew this was the man. I looked at the date he had joined Equally Yoked and found he had joined at the same time my mother had sent me the money to join—a month ago. I put all of his information up and left the building thinking, *"Okay, now that I have joined, God will tell him to call me."*

I waited until June without hearing anything. Finally, I stopped at Equally Yoked again, on my way home from work. I looked at his information again, and then I felt very strongly *I* should be the one to ask *him* to contact *me*. On June 20, I put in a request to let this man, Stuart, know I wanted to meet him. I felt a little strange asking a man for a date, but somehow I did it anyway because I felt so strongly about it. On June 24, I received a phone call from Stuart. Since I was on my way to a meeting, we could only talk for thirty minutes. We seemed to have a great deal in common. We had both been members of the same denomination almost all of our lives. We had the same moral and religious beliefs, and many of the same likes and dislikes. Our families were in the same social class. Most of all, I found out Stuart had a tremendous relationship with God. So, we started talking about answered prayers, healings, the Bible and our love for God.

We continued to talk by phone until July 6 when we finally decided to meet at my church for the Sunday morning service. After church, we both went home but continued to talk, only by phone again. Now, we talked more and more often until July 20 when we decided to go out on a date. By then, we were both totally convinced this was a God thing. Stuart, too, had been prompted by God to join Equally Yoked in April. He had done the same thing I had done. He joined but saw no one in the member's book he felt was right for him (remember, I hadn't joined yet). So he went home to wait for the right person to ask him out. He also told God he didn't want to date around. He just wanted God to point him to the right person. He told me he felt strongly he was not to ask anyone, that they would ask him. He had fifteen to twenty requests from ladies wanting to meet him, but he was sure none of them were right for him. He was wondering just where "God's Miss Right" could be.

As we talked, Stuart said he began to feel we were on the same spiritual level and that's why he kept calling back. He wanted to be very sure I was the one God had picked out before we went out on a date. By July 20, he said he was convinced I was God's choice. We went out on our first date that night. We went out to eat and then to a movie. As he took me home, he told me he knew God had put us together, and he knew we would be married soon. I was a little shocked he would say it that soon, but in my heart I knew he was right.

Even though I felt sure Stuart was God's choice, I asked God for one more thing, just so I could be positive. I asked Him to please have Stuart say to me, "I want you to know I love God more than anything else in my life. He will always be first." For some reason that seemed very important to me. I knew that's what went wrong in my first marriage. If Dan had only put God first, everything else would have worked itself out and there never would have been a divorce. I wanted to be sure Stuart was determined to always put God first in his life.

In the fall of 1996, Stuart sat down by me on my couch and looked very serious. He turned to look at me and said these words: "I don't want to hurt you, but I feel you should know you can never be first in my life. God will always be first, and you will be second. If it comes between something God tells me to do and something you want, it has to be God's way. I hope you can understand that." My insides were shaking by the time he finished. How much more proof could I ask for? God had truly handpicked Stuart to be my husband. He had put us together and shown me clearly this was His will.

We were married in October of 1996. My friend, Karen, insisted we not get married quietly, as Stuart suggested. She offered to plan the wedding, get the cake, punch, flowers and everything we needed to make it a memorable day. So we agreed. About thirty people crowded into Karen's living room for our wedding. It was a beautiful wedding, and I was happy she had talked me into waiting so I could have a wedding with friends and family.

Stuart was exactly what I needed for that time in my life. He encouraged me to think more highly of myself. My self-esteem was greatly lacking when I met him, but I became more and more confident. He was very self-confident, and it began to rub off on me. He also had confidence in my abilities. His words of encouragement and his love for me gave me such a strong sense of security. I grew much stronger because of him.

Another incident that happened showed how God was giving me so many things I had asked for in a man when He sent Stuart. I had asked God to please not give me a husband who wanted to change me. I knew who I was in God, and I liked myself—just as I was, just the way God made me. I had already been through a marriage where my husband continually wanted me to change the way I was, the way I dressed and the way I acted. Virtually everything about me was under attack by the time Dan left. It had felt so good to just be my own self for the past four years without anyone complaining. I needed to continue being my own genuine self.

Stuart told me God had instructed him to be careful to *not* try to change me. He said he wasn't supposed to make me change anything! I wasn't to do anything any differently than I had been doing it. During our entire marriage, he continually told me he loved me just as I was. He didn't want me to change anything. He didn't even want me to move the furniture or to move my clothes in the closet. He kept everything of his in a spare bedroom. He even used our guest bathroom. Nothing had to be changed when he moved into my townhouse. Stuart was *more* than accommodating to my needs.

Stuart also had great faith! And I mean ***great faith***! I thought I had faith, but I had never met anyone with the faith he had. He prayed several hours a day and was constantly in contact with God. He told me many times what he and God had talked about that day. It was truly amazing how close he walked with God. Many times, I would ask God in prayer to give Stuart the answer to something for me. It only took minutes for him to respond that he had heard from God with the answer. If I needed confirmation on something, I asked God to confirm it through Stuart, and I would be amazed at how quickly the confirmation would come.

I knew Stuart was definitely in tune with God—all the time. A good example of this was when I felt God was telling me we needed to change churches. We had been attending a church where I and my children knew the pastor quite well. Stuart was on the board of deacons at this church, and I wasn't sure what the pastor would think about us changing churches. So, I asked God to confirm we needed to make this move through Stuart, who was gone at the time. Within two hours of my prayer, he came through the door, picked up the phone directory and asked me the name of the church we heard about several months ago that had helped a single mom.

> *I thought I had faith, but I had never met anyone with the faith he had.*

I told him what it was, and he immediately said, "I believe we need to go there Sunday." It was the exact church I felt God urging me to go to. We attended the church the next Sunday, and we both agreed this was where we needed to be. Even though we knew no one at the church, we just knew we were supposed to attend there.

Another incident I remember quite vividly showed me how Stuart really listened to God. God seemed to tell him things, many times before they happened. I guess that's called "prophetic" in many circles. He definitely had that gifting. Our worship leader, whom everybody loved, was stealing money from the church and having an affair with the church secretary. Stuart told me for two months Richard was living in sin. He even mentioned it was as bad as adultery. He repeated it every Sunday until I told him to please quit ruining the service for me. I didn't want to think Richard was living in sin. It stopped me from concentrating on the worship service. Besides, no one else felt Richard was guilty of anything like that. He was a great Christian man. All Stuart would say was, "You'll see soon enough." Sure enough, he was right. The whole church was shocked when they learned what Richard had been doing.

No one could believe it. No one except Stuart, and he had known it for at least two months.

While I was married to Stuart, we both prayed for Dan. We knew my kids really needed a father who would love them and be able to talk about spiritual and fatherly things with them. They were still feeling so much rejection from their dad. We also talked sometimes about all the things that bothered me. I had such a hard time accepting all the bad things that had been told to me about Dan. One day, Stuart came in the door of our home, and he walked straight into the kitchen where I was. He said, "As I was praying for Dan today, I saw him praying and asking God for forgiveness. After he prayed, he changed drastically! He became such a great Christian man. You couldn't tell he had gone back on God. He was just as he was when he served God years ago." I was shocked! Somehow that gave me faith to believe there *was* still hope for Dan. Stuart and I both began praying for Dan's salvation that day. Stuart said, "He is not ready yet. He hasn't hit bottom, but he will."

Chapter 19

Is Healing for Everyone?

Over and over amazing spiritual things happened during my time with Stuart. I had never been that close to anyone with the prophetic gifting. In fact, I didn't even know there was a prophetic gifting. My church did not teach on that. I knew nothing about it, but I had heard of it, and I knew Stuart had it very strongly. For about a year, he had a dream over and over. He told me about the dream many times. He would wake up so excited he just couldn't quit talking about it. He said he was in Heaven, and he was with Jesus. He said other people were living all over Heaven and doing lots of other things, but he never left Jesus' side. Everywhere Jesus went, he went. He said all he wanted was to be close to Jesus' side all the time; and so he was. Other people didn't seem to care about being that close to Jesus as much as he did. They were perfectly happy wherever they were. He just loved Jesus so much he wanted to be near Him more than anything else. Stuart said every now and then he would go visit friends, and they'd ask him how it was up there by Jesus. He'd tell them how great it was, and they'd say, "We'll get up there to see you all sometime." The amazing thing was these people were also as happy as they could be. Everyone had exactly what they wanted. No one was jealous of anyone else or better than anyone else. Everyone was very content just as they were.

Then I would see Stuart just sitting in his recliner with big tears running down his cheeks, listening to a CD of "In The Garden." He loved the section about the dew on the roses, and also the chorus that says, "And He walks with me and He talks with me, and He tells me I am His own; and the joy we share as we tarry there, none other has ever known." He loved listening to that song, over and over again.

Stuart had this dream about Heaven so many times I began to wonder what was causing this dream. Also, he was so preoccupied with seeing Jesus and Heaven, he talked about it continually. He started telling me he wanted to be put in a Hospice House if he ever got sick and needed constant care. Next, he told me what he wanted me to do if he died. He told me what songs he wanted at his funeral, and he literally made all of his funeral plans. Finally one day, I asked him if we could please quit talking about dying. He said, "Oh, I'm not going to die anytime soon. I'm going to live to be an old man. I just think you should always be prepared and plan ahead for when the time does come." A while after that, I began to wonder if maybe *I* was the one who was going to die. God might be preparing me by giving Stuart this dream so I would start thinking about it. I thought maybe I should be making out a will, as well as funeral plans for myself. So I had my will made up, and I started thinking about things I needed to do before I died.

In February of 1999, Stuart had a complete physical because he had started to feel weak. They found nothing wrong except low iron in his blood count. The doctor put him on iron pills and told him to eat more red meat. He continued to get weaker and by April, the doctor decided to do a complete GI series—upper, lower plus twenty biopsies were taken. Nothing showed up, but yet, Stuart got weaker and weaker. By May, he was very weak, and he had a lump on his back. He took my advice and went back to see his doctor, who happened to be on vacation. An older, retired doctor was filling in for him. The retired doctor looked at Stuart and said, "You're not leaving this office today until I find out what's wrong with you!" He tried to lance what he thought was a cyst and found that it was not a cyst. It was cancer!

The doctor sent him for a chest x-ray and found spots on his lungs. Stuart was then sent to get a CAT scan. The CAT scan showed he had a large tumor in his kidney which had spread to his lymph nodes and his lungs. The Oncologist knew the cancer would soon spread to his bones, so they scheduled surgery to put a shunt in his chest with chemo drugs to halt the cancer. Everything was moving very quickly, but Stuart knew he had to pray before he did anything. He prayed very earnestly to know God's will in all of this immediately.

As Stuart prayed, he felt very strongly he should not keep the appointment at the hospital to have the shunt put in his chest. So, he cancelled it, and instead, he went to talk to his doctor. The doctor admitted the shunt would only postpone the inevitable. He told Stuart they might be able to give him a few more months to live, but no more than a year. The cancer had spread too far. It couldn't be stopped. At that point, he told the doctor he wanted to die naturally, not taking chemo or other drugs that would only postpone his death. The doctor then asked him if he wanted to be placed in Hospice care. Stuart agreed that's what he wanted. He had the doctor call Hospice, and they were to contact us right away.

Stuart asked to talk to me when I came home from work. He asked me to sit down, and he told me he knew I wouldn't like a decision he had made, but I needed to pray and turn it over to God. Then he told me he felt very strongly God was ready to take him home. Then he made me promise I would not pray for his healing. I did my best to pray with an open mind and seek God's will. It was so difficult to put aside my own will and truly seek God in this.

I had learned to depend on Stuart's love and companionship so much. As a prayer partner, he was so in tune with God! I thought about how I could pray and Stuart would confirm my answers so often. *How could I make it without him? I didn't want to give that up. We had become very close, due to our spiritual bond. How could I make it alone again? Why would God send him to me for only three years?* I had so many questions to work through. It was very hard, but God helped me continually as I sought to find His will in this all-important issue.

During this time in my life, I finally had to decide what my beliefs were on healing. I had struggled all my life with what I really believed about healing:

Will God heal anyone who asks Him for healing?

Does someone have to have faith before God will heal them?

Is illness caused by a mother or father wound, or bitterness over something that has happened to us? Do we have to get rid of these wounds and bitterness to be healed?

Is it God's choice or our own choice whether we are healed or not?

What about our beliefs? Does healing depend on our belief in God?

I had been around people all my life who felt very strongly each way. In my heart, I had been seeking to find the answer for myself since childhood.

When I was a child, my friend, Anita, had a grandfather who became very ill. George was a wonderful Christian, and we all loved him. He and his wife and family attended our church. We were good friends. Anita's grandmother, Louise, was a wonderful Christian, too, and a great prayer warrior. She started praying for her husband and told everyone she had the assurance God was going to heal him. Of course, everyone in our church became very excited and rejoiced with her, believing George would be healed.

Very shortly after that, George got worse and died. Everyone was shocked! With childlike faith, I believed with all my heart George was going to be healed. My faith was so strong I insisted on sitting on the very front row seat at his funeral. I wanted to be the first person to see him come up out of the casket. I just knew they would not bury George that day because God was going to heal him and raise him up. God could raise George from the dead if He wanted to. He had done it before with Lazarus. Anita's grandmother felt God had promised her George would be healed, and I knew God would keep His promise.

I waited with anticipation all through George's funeral. I sat on the edge of my seat. Finally, the funeral ended, and it was time to go to the cemetery. I was so disappointed. *Why didn't God heal George during the funeral?* Much to my disappointment, George was buried that day, and God did not raise him up out of the casket. I was totally crushed! *What happened? Why didn't God heal George? How could this be?* I was puzzled about this for days.

Finally, I asked my grandmother. She said, "Oh, George was healed. When God took him to Heaven, He healed him completely! He is now in perfect health in Heaven." In my mind, I thought, *"Wow! That seems to be a real cop-out. Would God really fool Louise and let George die?"* All of this was very confusing to me.

Another time, my grandmother told me to always be careful how I prayed. She said, "Do not pray for someone to be healed unless you are sure that it is in God's plan." Grandma then told me a story about a man named Chuck she had prayed desperately for God to heal. He was healed of a brain tumor, miraculously. Then he turned his back on God and became a terrible sinner. He was so much worse off than he had been in the first place. It would have been better for him to die earlier. Only God knew what was best. Grandma was sorry she had prayed for his healing. She felt she had misused her gift of healing. I thought, *"So I should always ask God what He wants? Like in the Garden of Gethsemane when Jesus prayed, 'Not My will but Thine be done' before He died on the cross?"* (Luke 22:42). I thought a long time about this. *What about all the people Jesus healed when He was on earth? Wasn't it God's will for all of them to be healed?* The Bible says Jesus healed all the sick who came to Him, except in the towns where there was a lack of belief in Him. It says, Jesus *"did not do many miracles there because of their lack of faith"* (Matthew 13:58, NIV).

I had pondered all of this over and over my entire life. Now I needed to decide. *Just what do I believe about healing? Are there times when God wants to receive glory from someone's dying? Not from their healing? And was Stuart's illness truly to be one of those times?* My heart was heavy, and I needed to hear from God on this for myself. What other people believed didn't matter now. I wanted to know what God was saying to me. I had to know how God wanted me to pray and what I was supposed to do now. It was no time for other people's opinions or theology. I had to hear directly from God, for myself, in order to weather this storm. Stuart said God had spoken directly to him, and he knew God was ready to take him home. *Could I argue with that? I had been learning every day for three years God did speak directly to Stuart—on many occasions. I had no doubt about that. But why would God want Stuart to go to Heaven so early? He was only 49.*

As I sought God's will, I also began to find out a few things that helped me to understand what God was doing. For one thing, the doctors told us Stuart had had this tumor for anywhere from three to five years. This meant he had this tumor when I met him. *Had God put Stuart and me together knowing he had a deadly tumor?* Then, I began to realize God knew all along Stuart was dying, yet He put us together for three years. I knew God had to have a reason for putting Stuart in my life, as well as putting me there for him.

Somehow, as I prayed, I began to hear God speak His will for me, and I surrendered my plans entirely to His. I knew God was going to take Stuart, and I had to accept this. We still live in a fallen world, and no matter how hard I wanted to change that, everyone was not going to be healed. It was only God's great Grace that had brought healing to me and my children on earlier occasions. This time, it was not going to happen. God was not extending that grace for Stuart's healing. I did as my grandmother had taught me. I did not pray for Stuart's healing since I did not feel it was God's will.

From that point, I followed my own heart and began to pray for God's Presence and His Peace during this time. I also prayed, "What do You want me to do now, God? What do I do after Stuart is gone?" Even though I was heartbroken, I knew beyond a shadow of a doubt God had a plan for me, though it was very different from what I had thought. In the middle of all my heartache and shock, I clearly heard God telling me to forget about myself. I was supposed to "Just take care of Stuart." God would take care of me when the time came. Right now, I was to forget about myself and think only of Stuart. I was here to help him get through this time as he prepared to die. I began to change my thinking totally. No feeling sorry for myself; every day was lived just to help Stuart.

Taking care of Stuart as he passed from this world to the next taught me so much! I could never have learned this any other way. God's Presence was so real during that time! He never left us nor did I doubt this was God's will for our lives. I felt as if God Himself was right there in the room with us, day after day and night after night. As Stuart worsened, Hospice decided to transport him to the Hospice House. They could see the cancer had spread through his bones and into his brain. He began to be irrational, and I couldn't convince him otherwise. Life at home became impossible for me. Also, at that time, they told me Stuart was nearing the end. It would be less than thirty days. While Stuart was being transported in an ambulance to the Hospice House, he became very confused and thought he was being kidnapped. I drove my own car to the facility, so I was not with him in the ambulance. When I got to the Hospice House, I saw Stuart with a wild look in his eyes. As I got closer to him, he warned me to be very careful. He said, "We have to figure out a way to get out of here. These people aren't who you think they are." I asked him why he thought that. He responded by looking at the TV. He said, "That's not a regular TV. None of the stations are normal. They are trying to brainwash me." The TV looked normal to me. I wasn't sure why he believed otherwise.

This idea of trying to escape continued on and on for quite some time in Stuart's mind. He continued to tell me we had to get out of there the first chance we could get. After a short time of trying to talk to him and getting nowhere, I didn't know what to do. I left the room for a few minutes to ask the director of the Hospice House what I should do. She and another advisor talked to me and told me they felt badly Stuart had gotten so confused. They could not make him stay if he wanted to leave or if I felt I should take him back home. At that point, I felt as if I were going to collapse. The stress of this whole situation was catching up with me. I prayed, "I just can't be strong anymore. God, help me!" I told the administrator and the other advisor I could not take Stuart back home again. I told them I needed to just wait a while and see if he would calm down. I went back to his room praying he would change his mind and begin cooperating with everyone. Up until then,

> When I was at the end of myself, God knew just the right person to send in.

he wouldn't even swallow his medicine or allow them to touch him. He was sure he had been kidnapped. He watched everyone very suspiciously waiting for a chance to escape.

As I sat at Stuart's bedside, the Hospice Chaplain walked through the door. She had a very calming temperament and soft voice. She wanted to pray with Stuart and see if there was anything she could do for him. He started talking to her. He began telling her about the TV brainwashing and about being kidnapped. Much to my surprise, he trusted the Chaplain! He listened to her as she turned the channels on his TV and explained to him how these were all the same channels on all TVs. There was CBS, NBC, MSNBC, local channels, Daystar™ and TBN. As she talked, I could see Stuart was calming down. He actually believed her! The wild look was leaving his eyes. God had heard my prayer of desperation. When I was at the end of myself, God knew just the right person to send in. As the Chaplain talked, Stuart listened. He was finally convinced he was in a hospital where the nurses and doctors were only there to help him. What a blessing that Chaplain was! She came at exactly the right moment! She was such a godsend! Finally, I could relax. I had help taking care of Stuart; we were staying!

Even though he was now convinced he was in a good hospital and they were actually helping him, not harming him, he was still a little suspicious about his medication unless I personally checked it out first. Nothing went into his mouth unless I explained what it was and that it was what he was supposed to have. Stuart even began to act irritated about his family. He truthfully trusted no one except me and the Chaplain. As the days went on, I had to stay right by his side, all day and all night. If he couldn't see me, I talked to him and told him what I was doing just to keep him calm. For one whole week, I never left the Hospice House. I stayed by his side. I was so glad for the plate glass window Stuart had in his room and the door which opened up to the outside. I could go out the door to get some fresh air and look at the woods behind the hospital. From there, I could still see Stuart in his bed. More importantly, he could still see me. It gave me some time to feel refreshed and still keep him calm.

Chapter 20

A Painful, Yet Priceless Experience

I played worship music much of the time I stayed in Stuart's room, I wrote in my journal, and I prayed. I wanted to be sure Stuart felt God's Presence very near. I also wanted to be sure Satan had no place in that room during the entire time we were there. Many people commented as they entered Stuart's room how they felt such great peace. I had the opportunity to give my testimony to so many people who came through that door. Finally, one day, I asked Stuart if he felt God's Presence or if it was getting tougher. He shook his head and muttered, "Better, Better!" I had no doubt then he was sensing God's Presence as I was. I was elated! Even though he could hardly talk to us, He was talking to God. I was so thankful. My whole purpose for that period of time was to make sure he was in God's Presence as he crossed over from this life to the next and he was.

As I sat watching Stuart's condition deteriorate each day, but sensing God's wonderful Presence, I began to lose contact with the outside world. Nothing mattered except what went on in that room. I sang, I prayed, and I bathed in God's Presence every day. God gave me such guidance, and I was never so completely at peace as I was during that last week of Stuart's life. I didn't want it to ever come to an end. It was a wonderful time with my Lord! Even though Stuart couldn't talk for his last few days, and he couldn't even open his eyes, it was just amazing to sit by his side and talk to him about the love of God. I knew his spirit knew and sensed God's Presence. I knew God was right there beside us, and it felt so good to bask in His Presence together.

On June 24, 1999, at 4:30 a.m., Stuart woke me up with a noise he always made to get my attention. It was a groan, since he hadn't been able to talk for several days. He wanted me to stand beside his bed. It was quite evident to me he was dying. Soon, I heard the death gurgle in his throat. I stood beside his bed, praying and sensing God was very near. I talked to Stuart as I stood there, rubbing his forehead and telling him I knew the end was near. I told him I felt God was very close, and I was going to be just fine. I was excited for him. He was truly going to go walk around Heaven with Jesus, just as he'd been dreaming about for a year now.

At around 8:30 a.m., Stuart opened his eyes very wide, he pulled up in his bed and said, "Oooh, oooh, oooh" over and over, and his eyes went from side to side as he looked up toward the ceiling. It was obvious to me we were not alone in that hospital room. Stuart was totally overwhelmed by what he saw up above us. His head went back and forth as he tried to take it all in. All he could say was, "Oooh, oooh, oooh" over and over. The look in his eyes was one of total amazement and unbelief. He looked happier than I had ever seen him—*ever!* Finally, his eyes fixed on one particular spot. He followed that one object across the ceiling and then down to his bedside. As he looked right through me, still following the object, he stopped breathing, and his head fell back on his pillow. During all of this, all I could say was, "Stuart, I wish I could see what you are seeing." I knew it must be a wonderful sight. I knew he must be seeing into Heaven and the angels were singing, and Jesus Himself was coming to get him. I felt sure only Jesus Himself could get Stuart that excited. He had dreamed and talked and imagined walking and talking with Jesus for so long. Finally, his dream was coming true. No wonder he was so excited!

After Stuart died, I stood unable to move for about a half hour. I just soaked up God's Presence. Finally, Stuart's brother, Gerald, came in. I believe he, too, immediately realized he was in God's Presence. He stood still beside the bed. Soon, two of my children came in. They also stood beside the bed recognizing God's Presence was there. We began to talk about Stuart's relationship with God and how much he loved Jesus. We all kept looking at his eyes. We could still see the amazement and excitement in them. No one wanted to leave God's Presence, but soon the nurse came in and asked us what time Stuart had passed on. The nurse gave us as much time as we needed. Visitors from the church came by, not realizing he had just passed away. They prayed with us as we held hands around the bed. It was actually a very warm, awesome time of praising God for Stuart's life and all he had meant to us.

I finally felt I was ready to talk to someone from the funeral home about arrangements. Gerald sat with me as we made arrangements for the funeral home to take Stuart. It was then I remembered Stuart had already told me throughout his last year exactly what I should do when he died. He gave me instructions about how he wanted everything handled. All I had to do was follow through with all he told me. I had very few decisions to make. They were already made for me. What a relief that was! I knew then God had been looking out for me all that year. He knew I wouldn't be able to think clearly after Stuart died. He also knew what Stuart would want done after he died. I would never have known what to do if he hadn't told me ahead of time, when he had a rational mind and was thinking very clearly. Stuart even told me he wanted our Care Group leader to preach his memorial service. He told me he wanted to be cremated and buried with me later. He told me about flowers and people he wanted at his service. About the only decision I had to make on my own was what type of frame I wanted to put Stuart's picture in for the service. That was tough enough! I was so glad God had prepared me so well for this extremely heartbreaking time in my life. Without His help, I would never have made it through all of that.

It was at this point, I was beginning to feel very numb and as if this were a dream. I felt like I wasn't really there; like I was just watching it all happen to someone else. I don't remember my trip home or what happened the rest of the day. At some point later, I know I told everyone the plans for Stuart's memorial service, but everything still seemed as if I was in a dream. I had very little sense of my own emotions or of what other people were saying or doing. In fact, it was very hard for me to actually pull myself back into the things of this world at all after that experience. I wasn't sure I *wanted* to go back to all the earthly things again. They seemed so futile. I'd been so enveloped in heavenly things! If it hadn't been for knowing my children and grandchildren needed me, I don't know if I would have been able to come back. I had a very strong sense of being called to help my family know God as I knew Him. That became my very reason for living.

This awesome experience took away my fear of death. Instead of fearing death, I thought of death as a time when I would be totally in the Presence of God where there is peace, joy and contentment this world could never comprehend. I had learned how the awesomeness of God's Presence takes away all fear.

Soon after his passing, God began to show me all the great things I had learned from Stuart. I had been in a classroom, studying the true meaning of faith. I had also learned about intercessory prayer and trusting God completely. I could easily see God had been teaching me the many things He wanted me to know. God knew how deeply I desired to be closer to Him. He placed Stuart in my life to teach me all the things I needed to know about loving Him and growing closer to Him. So, even though it was hard to lose Stuart, it was okay. I was just thankful God had given me those three years with him. How could I complain about the length of time I had with him? If God thought three years was long enough, it was long enough. I trusted His plan completely.

Something God revealed to me, quite some time later, was why we had to change churches just a short time before Stuart died. The church we had been attending was a good church, and we loved the pastor and the people there. In fact, when they heard how sick Stuart had been, they asked me and my daughter why we hadn't asked them to pray for his healing. They were devastated I hadn't called them. No matter how hard I tried to explain, I don't think they ever did understand why Stuart didn't want anyone to pray for his healing.

On the other hand, the church God moved us to, was going through a very similar experience to ours. One of their associate senior pastors had just lost his ten-year-old grandson and another couple in the church had just lost a teenage daughter. These people were searching for answers about why God chooses to heal some people and why He doesn't choose to heal others, just like I was. I remember thinking some of the sermons preached there were just for me. God knew where we needed to be in order for us to get through this season of our lives, and He placed us in the right church. I am so glad we listened to Him and didn't worry about what other people might think about us.

Many times, people who believe God heals everyone, anytime and anyplace cause grieving people to lose faith and even feel as though God failed them. Or they start doubting their own faith. However, if a person doesn't believe God still heals today, he actually misses out on so much of God's will for us as we live on this earth. God was teaching me something totally different from the beliefs of many of my friends. I had to work this out on my own and learn to just trust **Him**.

I recently heard a sermon that seemed to describe my final decision about healing. This is what I finally concluded: Jesus suffered and died on the cross for our salvation. We know we are saved by God's Grace. It's the same with healing as salvation; we are also healed by God's Grace. As He was going to the cross, Jesus was beaten so we could receive healing from our diseases. He paid the price for our healing, but it is by His Grace we are healed. That doesn't mean we won't have any sicknesses while we are here on earth. We live in a fallen world. If we do get sick, we can ask God to heal us by His great Grace. Our faith doesn't heal us, but we need faith to believe God when He says He wants to heal us and that He can.

Isaiah 53:5 (NKJV)
But He was wounded for our transgressions, He was bruised for our iniquities; the chastisement for our peace was upon Him, and by His stripes we are healed.

The many times in my life, when God wanted to heal me, He asked me to do something, showing I had faith to believe He could heal me. Faith was not the issue in Stuart's case. We both believed God could and would heal him unless He had a better plan, which He did. God wasn't mean to Stuart or to me by saying He wasn't going to heal him. God, in His great Wisdom, decided it was time for Stuart to come Home now, to come walk with Him. Once we were convinced of God's will, we

> *We know we are saved by God's Grace. It's the same with healing as salvation; we are also healed by God's Grace.*

had to trust Him. He is never wrong. God did not choose to heal Stuart by His great Grace. He decided it was better for Stuart to live in Heaven. It's just like what it says in Paul's writings: *"For me to live is Christ and to die is gain"* (Philippians 1:21).

I may never know why Stuart had to die at such a young age. I do know God wanted me to be there to witness how sweet that death was for His precious saint. Now, I am totally convinced death really has no sting and dying truly can be a wonderful experience for those who *live in Christ*. Stuart's dying was a priceless experience for me! I wouldn't exchange it for anything. That one experience caused my faith to grow by leaps and bounds. It brought me into a whole new understanding of God's Love. It also gave me a new determination to teach everyone I know about that great, great Love.

Life after Stuart's death was much harder than I had anticipated. Everything reminded me of him. In order to get through this, I decided to clean out his closet and give his clothes to the Salvation Army. I knew he'd like that. Next, I moved things in the house that were reminding me of him. After a few months, I was still having trouble. Even though I knew where Stuart was, I still missed him so much. I finally had to take his pictures down, which I didn't really want to do, but I knew I needed to, at least for a while. This helped me quite a bit, but I still burst into tears frequently when I was reminded of him. This went on for about a year. I think it was very natural, but it seemed very painful to me, and I hadn't expected it to be quite so hard.

Just six weeks after Stuart passed away, my first granddaughter, Hope, was born. She was my fourth grandchild. I had three boys: Kevin, Cory, Josh and now Hope. This should have been a wonderful experience, but my emotions couldn't quite make the switch from grieving to being ecstatic over having my first granddaughter. Stuart had been so excited we were having a granddaughter. Seeing her reminded me so much of Stuart I had trouble enjoying it. I went back and forth from happy to sad, happy to sad. I felt like I was on a roller coaster,

> *Our faith doesn't heal us, but we need faith to believe God when He says He wants to heal us and that He can.*

and I became emotionally exhausted. I wanted to be happy, yet inside I was still grieving and couldn't enjoy the experience as I had hoped I would. I know my son and daughter-in-law wondered what was wrong with me. Most people have trouble truly understanding grief until they actually go through it themselves. It's one of those things "you have to experience" to understand.

Chapter 21

Are You Scamming Me?

Shortly after the new baby was born, and about three months after Stuart's death, something happened that confused me even more. Dan started calling me, and then he came back to Texas for a visit. He told me he felt through Stuart's death, God was giving him another chance to make things right. That is, if I would take him back. He said he wanted to go to church with me and the kids and get his life turned around. He said he realized now how wrong he'd been, and he was so thankful for this second chance. He even got a good job close by as a mobile home salesman. It really did appear he was doing quite well, in every way. *Had Dan repented as Stuart had prophesied? Were things to be just as they had been before he went back on God?*

Since my emotions weren't normal, and I wasn't thinking clearly, I started wondering if this could be true. *Could God actually be giving Dan a second chance? Was he ready to be a good husband and father? Had he truly been seeking forgiveness from God?* I talked to Dan and met him at church on Sundays and to go out to dinner. We also started getting together as a family again by having family parties and going out to eat together, etc. I could tell the kids felt good having us all together again.

I told Dan I had forgiven him. I thought I could prove that to everyone by never bringing anything up again. I even told him I really loved Thomas and would have no problem raising him as my own if that's what he wanted to do. I knew I could do that because Thomas and I had a special bond. I really did love him. I felt so good knowing God had taught me how to truly forgive. In some ways, this experience was very good for me. It made me realize just how far I had come from the days of unforgiveness that were totally gone now.

However, I soon began to sense something just wasn't right. I couldn't put my finger on it. One thing I found very hard to deal with was Dan expected me to totally forget about Stuart, as if he had never existed. Of course, I couldn't do that no matter how hard I tried. I tried to stifle my emotions because it irritated Dan when I mentioned Stuart, even though he had only died just four months earlier. At one point, Dan said, "I can't be Stuart!" which showed me he had no idea what I was feeling. It also let me know I wasn't hiding my true feelings very well. I told him I didn't want him to be Stuart, but he didn't seem to understand. I couldn't wipe the last three years of my life out. I didn't even want to.

The thing that really bothered me the most was how Dan talked about the family he left in Georgia as if *they* were his family. My children and I could very easily see Dan missed his new family very much. He couldn't hide it. The tone in his voice when he talked about them was very loving. We all knew he longed to be with them. I also started noticing Dan was becoming more critical and demanding of me. I had such a great marriage with Stuart. I wasn't accustomed to being treated like Dan was treating me. I started to realize our relationship was not at all what I wanted *or needed*. I became very oppressed and unhappy.

Only God knew how to help me at that time. I started wondering, *"Was this for real? Was I really supposed to go back to Dan and forgive and forget? Was I supposed to return to that marriage where I had felt so inadequate?"* I told God I would do that if it was His will, but I was feeling oppressed and confused. I needed Him to show me what He wanted me to do. I started praying very desperately for God to help me and make His will clear to me. My desires and plans were only that I find God's perfect will for my life. I had no agenda of my own.

In less than six weeks, Dan began to show he was not at all interested in making things right with me *or* God. He started acting just like the man who left us seven years before. I don't know if he came to see me with good intentions and then changed his mind, or if he came knowing we would never get together again. About four or five weeks after he returned, Dan asked me to buy a mobile home for us to live in the country, about thirty miles away from where I was living at that time. He said his credit was still bad, and he couldn't buy the trailer himself. This was much farther from my work, my church, our children and our four grandchildren. It was away from everyone I knew. I told him I didn't really want to live that far out. I had a nice home, and I liked living there. He told me my townhouse was just too small. He didn't think he could live there. If we were going to get together, we needed a larger place to live; a double-wide trailer out in the country would be great for us. When I compared the two homes, I thought they seemed very much alike, except in the living room and kitchen area. The mobile home did have more room to have company over and to cook in the kitchen. I wondered if maybe that was why Dan didn't like my townhouse. I didn't know. I just knew he didn't like it. Still, to move thirty miles away from everything didn't make sense to me.

I was well aware I was still not thinking clearly and my emotions were very much on edge. I also knew I had prayed and asked God to help me think more clearly and do what He wanted me to do. I didn't want to throw away a chance to have my family all back together again—if God truly *was* giving Dan a second chance. I just couldn't make sense of why I needed to move so far away from everything I wanted to be close to. So, I told him I didn't want to live that far out. There was no reason for me to buy a mobile home thirty miles farther away from my work and church. He said, "Your credit is good, and I think it would be a good investment for you, even if you don't want to live in it. Why don't you just buy it for me? I really like it."

When he said this, I became even more confused than ever. *So, he wanted to live thirty miles away? What was he going to do out there, away from me, the kids, his work and church?* Then he started pushing me very hard to sign the papers and apply to buy this home for him. Dan was sure everything would be approved. He would pay me rent each month, so I wouldn't have to worry about monthly payments. He promised to sign a contract with me, and we could get it notarized. He said I could hold the contract in case he ever missed a payment; then I could kick him out.

I told him I was already in the process of getting my townhouse transferred into my own name. My mother and father wanted it to be in my name. I had to have my credit checked for that loan first. I'd be getting this taken care of very soon. I didn't want to try to do both at the same time. I didn't think my salary would be enough to get both loans approved. At that, Dan said, "Oh, you can do both! Just be sure you do the mobile home first. After that, you can do the townhouse. You should start the mobile home paperwork right away." I thought, *"Now that would be crazy! Why would I take a chance of losing the opportunity to own my own townhome that I love, so I can buy a mobile home I don't even want?"* Nothing he said was making good sense anymore. I knew something was very wrong. I began to sense I needed to put an end to this conversation. Something was definitely not right!

All at once, I started thinking clearly and everything started to come together for me. I asked Dan, **"Are you wanting me to buy that trailer so you can bring your other family here to live?!"** He said, "Why should that matter to you? You'd be getting paid every month, and it would be a good investment for you." I was shocked! I immediately told him I had no intention of buying a mobile home for him to bring his second family here to live in. At that point, he became very upset, and I could tell he was *very* angry with me. I looked at him and thought, *"He's not here because God gave him a second chance. How could I have been so fooled?"* I was so glad God helped me to see through all of this. It was so hard for me to believe Dan would try to trick me into going into debt to purchase a home for him and his new family! I had worked so hard to get myself financially straightened out after he left. And to think he would take advantage of me at a time like this made it even worse. He *knew* I'd be vulnerable and not in my normal state of mind after Stuart's death. Dan had been a pastor. He, himself, had counseled widows on ***not*** making decisions too soon after their husband's death. This was such a tough lesson for me to learn at that time in my life.

I was reminded again of the scripture God had given Sarah on the day Dan was leaving. The last part of it said I was, ***"Never to be entangled again by this bondage."*** God reminded me I was to never fall into this trap again. **He was freeing me from Dan "forever."** That helped me so much! No matter what, I knew my relationship with Dan was to be over—for good. Why had it taken me seven years to see that? God was so good to me, even when I was confused and my mind was not at its best. He stepped in and stopped me from making a very *BIG* mistake.

Dan was staying with Sarah while he was getting settled here. He went home that evening and told her he had made a mistake in coming here. He thought he wanted to have his family back together again, but now he realized I was still just as selfish as always. He told her he had given me a test just to see what I'd do, and he found I hadn't changed at all. He couldn't make this work with me as selfish as I was. He was going to try to transfer out of this area; he didn't want to live here anymore. Sarah didn't tell me what all Dan said until quite some time later. I think she was crushed. She thought I'd done something that hurt her dad very badly. I began to feel a coolness come between us. It was several months later when I explained to her what had actually happened. She had no idea!

Soon, Dan transferred to another city southwest of Dallas and brought his new family with him there to live. He was doing very well financially, and he decided to make that his new home. He met with me at a restaurant before he left to let me know he was doing great at his new job, and he would be very well off financially. He didn't need anyone to help him. **He told me all he needed was money. He didn't need God! Money was all that was important to him, and he was going to have it now.** He told me he was **tired of doing right**. Now, he was going to live for himself and do what *he* wanted to do.

A man who knew God's Word extremely well allowed Satan to strip his memory of all God had given him.

He was very loud and very rude. I was embarrassed at how people around the restaurant were looking at him as he was talking so loudly. As he talked, I wondered how I could have been so blind to think he had changed or God had sent him back to give our marriage a second chance. I was so glad to be able to get away from him. I saw very little of him for several years after that meeting.

Finally, after my mind became clear, I realized Dan probably thought I had received insurance money after Stuart's death, and he had checked my credit to see if I could borrow money. He just wanted my help to get him and his other family moved to this area. I was just a stepping stone to get him where he wanted to go. I never did find out if he was being honest when he first arrived or if he was scamming me the whole time. I thanked God so much for helping me to have the sense to say, "No."

A year or two after Dan moved south of Dallas, he had a stroke. He was placed on disability permanently. He and his second family moved back to Georgia to be close to her family. He hasn't worked since. He has had one illness after another since the stroke: heart disease, diabetes, serious digestive problems and now Parkinson's Disease. It's been sad to watch him learn the hard way that God's plan is always the best plan. When we know His plan and directly disobey, we never win.

I think one of the saddest things about this whole experience was to think about what could have been. Dan had a tremendous anointing from God to preach and win souls for God's Kingdom. God had given him an unusual gifting others would have been thrilled to have. Why he would walk away from that gifting and anointing and think he could make it on his own is more than I can fathom. Satan was so deceiving in convincing Dan he'd be better off doing what he wanted rather than following God's plan for his life.

A man who knew God's Word extremely well allowed Satan to strip his memory of all God had given him. He became so different. His once good heart became selfish. He used his very influential personality to scam people rather than win hearts to God. I know God's heart must have hurt more than mine. I still pray God will somehow turn Dan around so he can see Him once again. Even though he has lost so many years of winning souls, I pray he at least will save his own soul by choosing God. As Stuart prophesied, I pray one day Dan repents, and it will be as if he never went back on God.

Chapter 22

Are You Sure?

After Stuart died, I continued to attend the same church for one year. After that year, I noticed I was still sitting in the same seat I had always sat in when Stuart and I went there. I was still around the same friends we had while we went to church. But I couldn't sit in Stuart's seat. I always scooted over, and I sat on the second seat from the end. I cried all during the morning service just thinking about Stuart's passing one year before. So, on that one-year anniversary of Stuart's death, I decided I needed to make a change. I needed to start going to church with my daughter, Sarah. I felt like it would help me to be able to start over again and quit living in the past where Stuart and I had so many memories. I talked to Sarah that week, and she was happy to have me go to church with her and her two boys. Her husband worked a lot of Sundays, so I could be a big help to her, as well as be able to change my surroundings and quit grieving so much. She thought it was a great idea. So in July 2000, I started attending a new church close to my daughter's house. Even though it was quite a way for me to drive, it would be worth it if it helped me get through my grieving.

Sarah had moved into a new home just a few months before Stuart died. In fact, Stuart had been responsible for praying and interceding for Sarah's new house. He even described it to her before she found it. She wanted to go to a church closer to her new home. She had a friend who attended there, so that's where we went. The boys loved the Children's Church and Sarah really liked the pastor and the great music program. It seemed like the perfect match for her family.

I soon began to be happy I had changed churches. Everything was new for me. I enjoyed being with my daughter and grandchildren, too. About that same time, my oldest son, Daniel, and his family decided to move and attend the church with us. (After my son, Mark, graduated from college and moved home, he, too, started attending our new church.) It was great to be surrounded by my family again during church services. I began to feel very comfortable there and even made friends with the pastor. His father had also been a pastor who had gone back on God, just as Dan had. We talked about it several times. Somehow, it created a bond between us. I felt like I had someone who understood my children's confusion about their father (who had also been their pastor). He also had an understanding of all I had lived with for several years. Our pastor was a great friend to us. He had a very understanding heart. I felt God put all of us in this pastor's church for a reason.

When Mark graduated from college, I went to his graduation which was up north in Minnesota. He and his wife had decided they wanted to move back to Texas and find jobs once Mark finished college and before he entered law school. So, I helped Mark load up his truck and head to Texas with me the day after graduation. The plan was for Mark to find a job in the Dallas area and then send for his wife to come down. She would continue at her job until Mark had a job to provide for them. Mark was going to live with me until he had a steady job, then his wife would move here, too.

The day after Mark and I got back to Dallas, Sarah delivered my second granddaughter, Bethany. Now we had two girls and three boys. Excitement was high, and I was allowed to be in the delivery room. There is nothing to compare with watching a baby being born! The awesomeness of God's plan for creation is made so real. I could hardly control my emotions as I saw this new life come into our world. It reminded me of how much higher God's ways are above our ways. We cannot fathom His mind, His ways or His plans. We serve a great, great God. I spent the next year helping Sarah with her three small children and Daniel's two little ones.

Things didn't work out for Mark and his wife, and he ended up living with me as he went through his heartbreaking divorce. It was so hard hearing him sobbing night after night as he tried to seek God for strength to make it through each day. Mark loves deeply, and he just couldn't give up nor believe his marriage could end after only five years. He was in total shock. Helping him through that whole year was very stressful, but I knew he truly needed me. I understood his pain, for sure.

It was during that year Mark and I leaned hard on God and each other. God did not fail us. Just as He had been there in the past, His Presence was with us through another setback. His love was so real! Though it was very hard to see him so heartbroken, I was well aware God used this heartache to draw Mark closer to Him. Mark's faith and love for God grew unbelievably during that tough time as he turned to God for comfort and peace. He even saw angels in his room one night, dancing and singing. The Lord helped us get through that experience with a renewed faith and trust in Him. It never ceases to amaze me how pain and heartbreak seem to bring us to the feet of Jesus. We learn so much from Him during those times of brokenness. Could it be our brokenness can actually help us to find the relationship with God we so desire.

In 2002, almost three years after Stuart died, Sarah and I were sitting in church one Sunday morning, and she showed me the church bulletin. She pointed out there was going to be a church Valentine's social for people over 50. She thought I should get out more and start being around other people. For three years, I hadn't gone to anything except church services, a Care Group (I had just joined) on Thursday evenings and family get-togethers. Sarah wanted me to begin having a social life again. She thought it would really be good for me. As I read the church bulletin, I saw where it said the social was for "couples over 50 years of age." I pointed that out to Sarah, and she looked sad but shook her head as if to say, "Okay." The next Sunday we were sitting in the church service, and I looked at the bulletin. This time, the bulletin had been changed to read that the Valentine's social was for "couples and singles over 50." Wow! How did they know I wanted to come to the social? Sarah noticed it, too. I looked at her and nodded my head that I'd think about going now that I was also included in the invitation.

It never ceases to amaze me how pain and heartbreak seem to bring us to the feet of Jesus.

All that week, as I thought about the social, I had a very strange sense of urgency. I felt like I was supposed to go to this Valentine's Party. So, when it came time to go to the party, I got in my car and headed to the church. On my drive there, I prayed and told God I knew He was urging me to attend this social. I didn't know why. As I prayed about it, I felt very strongly God had someone He wanted me to meet that night. I asked Him to make it clear to me who it was.

It was a fun party. We played games, ate and had a great time of fellowship. While I was there, a couple I knew invited me to their Care Group on Sunday evenings. I had just started attending the Thursday night Care Group which this couple attended also. They said they attended two groups and really loved both. So, I thought I would do the same thing. After all, I had the time to attend two groups. It was the only activity I was participating in. At the end of the Valentine's Party, a gentleman from the Care Group invited me to go out to eat with the group. They were going out for Chinese food. I love Chinese food but had promised to bring my grandson, Cory, some candy after the party that evening. So, I gave him my excuse and did not go out to eat with the group. Actually, I was very nervous since it was my first social in three years. I felt much more comfortable going to my daughter's house to see my grandkids than going out to eat with people I had just met. At that point, I felt sure I'd accomplished what God wanted me to do that evening. I had that sense of peace from Him.

I started attending the Sunday evening Care Group and enjoyed it very much. As I attended and got to know the people better, they started announcing group activities like eating out, going to the "Passion Play" and other activities where we could go fellowship and have a good time. I really began to feel comfortable with all the people in the group, and they became my good friends. Every time we went to an activity, it seemed I was paired up riding and sitting with the same person. He was a single man named Robert, the same one who had invited me to go eat with the group that first night we met at the Valentine's Party. We were becoming very good friends and even sat together at the Care Group meetings.

As we attended group meetings, I could feel he had a heart that sought after God. He had been a Christian for only four years and had just moved to the Dallas area from California. Somehow, his hunger to do God's will and the way he talked about reading the Scriptures and seeking God, really got my attention. In my heart I thought, *"This is a man who really loves God and is putting God's will above his own desires."* He even expressed his desire to know if God would approve of him remarrying. His wife of 27 years had asked him to move out of their home because she didn't want to be married any longer. She filed for divorce and even though he didn't want the divorce, he had no choice. So, did the Bible say he could remarry or should he remain single the rest of his life? He was so sincere about this. I knew he was determined to do whatever God told him to do, even if it meant he had to live alone the rest of his life. I could tell Robert truly was seeking God with all of his heart. He was honest, sincere and very hungry for God.

I began to wonder if Robert might be the reason I went to the Valentine's Party and also the reason I was in this second Care Group. Finally, I asked God to clearly show me if Robert was the reason He had sent me to the party. I was pretty sure I already knew the answer, but up until now, I hadn't felt much interest coming from Robert to me. We were clearly just friends.

After a few months of knowing each other, Robert invited me to go out to eat—just the two of us. The pastor mentioned a restaurant named Babe's in his sermon one Sunday morning. That evening at Care Group, Robert asked me if I'd like to go there for dinner next Sunday after church. I thought it sounded like a great place, so I accepted his invitation. That week, I kept wondering just exactly what this invitation meant. I was wondering if Robert wanted this to be a date or were we just friends going out to eat after the church service?

I started getting excited as Sunday came around. I went to the same church service I always went to: 11:15 a.m. I got there five minutes early so I could find Robert. As I looked around the vestibule, I couldn't find him anywhere. I stopped at the kiosk where our Care Group leader's wife was working. I asked her if she'd seen Robert come by, but she said she hadn't. So I looked around a little longer but realized the service was starting, so I went on into the sanctuary and found a seat. As I looked around the sanctuary, I didn't see Robert anywhere. Then I started thinking about how he is *always* on time everywhere he goes. If he was coming today, he'd have been here by now. I wondered what could be wrong.

After church, I looked around again, but Robert wasn't there. I went on home and back to my regular routine. When it came time to go to Care Group, I wondered what Robert would say. *Or, had he totally forgotten about our date?* All evening, Robert said absolutely nothing. I went home thinking, *"How inconsiderate. Robert asked to meet me for lunch then forgot all about it."* That made me very sure he and I were still just friends. If Robert had been asking me out for a date, he wouldn't have forgotten about it. I began to wonder if I had misunderstood about Robert and me.

A couple of weeks later, driving to Care Group, I asked God to have Robert show some indication he cared about me. I really wanted to know for sure he was the reason I was at this Care Group. Just some type of affection or special notice was all I asked for. Up to that point, there had been absolutely no affection or sign of caring shown to me by him. During prayer request time, I requested prayer for my granddaughter, Bethany, who had just been diagnosed with scoliosis. During prayer that night, Robert reached over and held my hand all during the prayer. He had never done that before. As he did that, I seemed to hear God say, *"Okay, that's your sign Robert really does care about you."* I thought, *"Thank You, God. I was just making sure."*

After that, I felt much more confident God was in charge, and He knew what He was doing. Maybe how long it took was not important to God. Maybe He just wanted us to be together in the Care Group for now. I was learning a whole lot about Robert and seeing more and more how much he loved God. I was becoming much more comfortable with him as God showed me how we could help each other and serve Him together. I thought it was actually a great way to get to know someone quite well before they could ever try to impress you. Maybe God planned it this way.

By the time Robert asked me out on an actual date, I felt like I knew him very well, and he knew me, too. A spiritual connection is a very real bond that pulls two people together as friends or as spouses. Robert and I were very connected spiritually as we continued to attend Care Group. We began to talk more and more as the months went by. Finally, we exchanged phone numbers just in case we needed to reach each other. We prayed for each other's needs and even spoke on the phone off and on about our prayer requests. We were just good friends for seven months.

One day, Robert came home from a week of traveling. I saw him at church, and I could tell he was very upset. I felt very strongly I should call him and see if he needed to talk. He agreed, and we met at a local restaurant. Robert was concerned about his job and was going to start applying for other jobs around the country. He told me he was going to Tennessee for an interview within the next few weeks. He was taking vacation time from his present job in order to do this. I was a little confused with what he told me but agreed to pray for him. We exchanged email addresses so we could keep in touch if we needed to.

Robert went back on the road to work and then to Tennessee for his one-week vacation while he interviewed for a new job. I was home asking God if He was sure Robert was the right man for me. I told God if Robert moved away from here, I probably would never even see him again—unless he called or visited or something. Even then, I didn't want to move away and leave my children and grandchildren. They had been so helpful while I was going through all my tough times. I had grown very close to all of them. *Would God be asking me to move?* No, I felt very comfortable God did not want me to move. *So, what about Robert? How did this all fit together?*

As the days flew by, I continued to pray for Robert and his job. Finally, after not hearing anything for quite some time, I asked God to give me one more sign I wasn't wrong about Robert and he was still the man God had for me. I said, "God, if Robert is the man You want me to marry, please have him call me just so I will know he's still the one." As I said that prayer, I was a few miles from my house. I drove on home and walked in my front door. I could see my answering machine was flashing. I had a message from a call I had just missed. As I turned the machine on, I heard this message: "Hi, this is Robert. I'm not really sure why I'm calling. I just felt like I needed to call you now. You can call me back." Robert had called me, just as I had asked God to have him do. He didn't even know why he was calling. God had just nudged him to call.

How good God is! He gave me another sign. I had no doubt now. I knew God still wanted me to be with him. He would work it all out.

I called Robert back only to find he felt the interviews had gone very well. He was encouraged that he might have gotten the job and was anxiously awaiting a call from the company soon. The company head of sales and the owner had all but told Robert he had the job. He was tired from all the interviews, and he was glad he was finally finished. He would be home in just a day or so. He had even driven to Florida for a final interview with the owner before they hired him. What could God be planning? Robert is moving to Tennessee, and I'm supposed to stay here in Dallas? Yet, God wants me to be with Robert? Nothing was making sense to me. All I knew to do was ask God to bring His plan into being. I started praying for myself and for Robert. I asked God to please make this all work out for His Glory. I began to have a very strong feeling he would not be getting that job in Tennessee—even though he thought he was just as good as hired.

He returned home and continued to work at home and attend Care Group. Before long, he told me the company he had interviewed with had changed their minds. They decided not to hire anyone. He was quite distraught he had spent so much time interviewing with them and using his vacation and money only for them to decide they didn't need anyone else. However, he still had a lot of work to do on his present job while he continued to look for other employment. As he told me what happened, I knew God was working out His plans for Robert, but I didn't say a word to anyone. I just continued to pray God would reveal His plan to Robert in the right timing. I wasn't sure why he was still in the dark about our relationship, but I knew God always has perfect timing. So, I just waited, trying to be patient.

On a Sunday in late September, while sitting in church, God revealed His plan to Robert. As we were sitting in church with our Care Group, we started singing the song, "Open My Eyes, Lord." Robert looked down the row and saw me. He later said, "All at once, a light came on as I looked at you. It was as if I was seeing you for the first time." He said he became aware immediately I was the perfect mate for him. He describes it as God opening his eyes as we were singing, "Open My Eyes, Lord." This was a new experience for Robert, and he became quite overwhelmed.

Rather than ask me out face to face, Robert decided to send me an email. He thought it would be much easier to take a second rejection by email than on the phone or face to face. (We still hadn't talked about the Sunday we were supposed to go to Babe's together.) He emailed me and asked me to go to the Texas State Fair with him that next Saturday. I was surprised to see the message and responded to it right away. Of course, I'd go to the fair with him. I started wondering, *"Is this a real date? Had Robert finally realized we were supposed to be together?"*

On Saturday, Robert came to my house to pick me up. He met my son, Mark, and my oldest grandson, Kevin, as he came in. We talked for a few minutes, and then we were off to the fair. As we walked up to the ticket booth at the fair, Robert opened his billfold and turned to me and said, "Now is this a date? Or are we just two friends going to the fair together?" I knew from the look on his face he wanted to get it straight, too. *Are we actually dating now? Robert had always paid my bill for everything we'd done together up to this time. Why would he act like he might not pay now?* I answered him right away. "I think I would like for this to be a date." Robert smiled very big. I knew by that smile I had given the answer he wanted to hear. As we walked around the fair grounds, he reached over and took my hand. We both immediately felt a strong electrical shock when our hands touched. We still talk about how amazing that was. We had such a great time all day. That evening, as we stood around the stage area, Alan Jackson was singing, "Somebody Loves You." Robert leaned up and gently kissed me on the back of my head. I immediately felt like my body was tingling all over. I couldn't believe it was actually happening. God had again brought a wonderful man into my life to love me and be my constant companion. Robert was perfect; God knew he would be. He had moved him from California to Texas—just for me! What a caring, loving God I serve!

Robert and I talked about several things that day—one being the Babe's restaurant date we never had. I didn't know Robert had been attending the 9:00 a.m. church service. I always attended the 11:15 a.m. service. Neither of us thought to ask the other which service we would meet at. He thought I had stood him up at the 9:00 a.m. service, so he waited until 11:00 a.m. thinking I might be coming to the later service. Just before the 11:00 a.m. service started, he left the church feeling very hurt, thinking I wasn't coming. Robert always went to church early. He didn't realize I walk in just in time for services. We evidently just missed each other. He was probably leaving as I pulled up. I'm sure it was all about God's timing. God knew the perfect time hadn't come yet for us to get together. Now, at the end of September 2002, it was time.

Robert took me home that evening and kissed me goodnight at my door. He asked if he could pick me up for church the next morning, and of course, I said, "Yes." I slept very little that night. I was so excited to begin this next new phase of my life. It was hard to believe it was actually happening! I thanked God over and over for His love and care. I felt very special to God. He had been so faithful to me. I was anxious to know what God had in store next for Robert and me.

The next day, we went to the 11:15 a.m. service at church and sat together as a couple for the first time. After church, we went out to eat and then to visit my daughter and her children. They all *loved* Robert. Next, he took me to his house to show me where he lived. He showed me all around the house and yard and then came back into the living room. He had very little furniture because he was gone most of the time traveling, so the living room was empty except for a recliner and a TV. He turned as we walked into the living room and said, "I know what I want in my life. I want to marry you. Do you want the same thing?" I looked at him in surprise. I couldn't believe he was saying this only one day after our first date. I did know marrying Robert was God's will and what I wanted very much, so I said, "Yes, that's what I want, too."

He was ready to elope to Las Vegas that very night. I, however, felt I couldn't leave my payroll job and run off to get married without giving some type of notice. I was afraid I'd have no job to return to when I came home. Who would cut paychecks for the 800 hourly people I was responsible to pay that week? I was sure they were all expecting checks and probably needed them. I didn't want to let them down. Besides that, I knew my children would want to see us married. We had all become so close the past few years. I just couldn't do something so important and life-changing without them being there.

From that day on, for the next six weeks, we dated and visited family and talked about getting married. We were just looking for the right time. Robert was also concerned he might be losing his job soon. He was still looking, but so far he hadn't found anything that seemed right. We finally decided to go ahead and get married rather than wait until he started a new job and couldn't take time off work. We wanted to spend a few weeks together anyway before he went back on the road again. So, we had a few friends over and were married in Robert's backyard. He had two palm trees overhanging his backyard deck. It made the perfect setting for a wedding. I actually enjoyed buying the cake and making arrangements for the wedding. It was the first time I had been able to pick out my own cake and have what I wanted at a wedding. I did everything exactly as I wanted it. It was very exciting and fun!

We planned a very small, intimate wedding, but ended up having thirty people in the backyard! Some of our Care Group friends just couldn't stay away. They said they felt they just had to crash the wedding and be there. I took a week off work for our wedding and to move my belongings into Robert's house. It was a great week! Robert's brother, Richard, came from California just to meet me and help us move. He was a big help. We moved my things all day and played games during the evenings until we finally had everything moved.

After that, Robert spent time getting my townhouse ready to put on the market. He enjoyed being a handyman, and I was so glad to have him at home each evening. The grandsons called him "Bob the Builder." We were both dreading the time he went back on the road.

Finally, Robert decided he didn't want to go back on the road. He was very tired of traveling all over the world. He started looking for a job where he could be home each evening. In March, he went to work for a bank, right in our area. He never had to go back on the road again. We were both so happy God helped us be able to spend more time together. We had so much fun! Robert liked to read to me in the evenings, and we began to get very involved in a new church.

Just a few months after we were married, my son, Mark, had visited a new little church that was temporarily meeting in a daycare center, and he liked it. He asked us to go with him one Sunday to see what we thought. We felt so at home on that first visit. We both felt we had found our new church home as a couple. And we both knew it was where God was placing us for this season of our lives. We have been going there for twelve years now. It has been a place where we have grown spiritually and individually, as well as in our marriage.

Soon after we started attending our new church home, I told Robert I felt very strongly I'd be working at our new little church one day on a full-time basis. I didn't know when. The church was still pretty small, and there weren't many employees. Somehow, I just knew one day God would place me in a full-time job there. Meanwhile, Robert and I volunteered to teach and pray and do whatever we could to be a blessing. It's always exciting to serve God wherever He places us.

Chapter 23

Oh, No! This Can't Be Happening!

In July of 2003, I was on my hour and a half commute to work when my cell phone rang. It was Robert. He thought he might be having a heart attack. I immediately felt my body going into shock. I was tingling all over and everything seemed like it was happening in slow motion. "Call 911 now!" I told him. He said he was going to as soon as he hung up. I was too far away to get home quickly, so I called Sarah. She drove straight to our home and arrived just as the ambulance was putting Robert inside. Sarah jumped inside the ambulance and began to pray for God to take care of Robert and send angels to minister to him. She asked God to please heal Robert and let nothing bad happen to him. Then the ambulance took him away to the hospital.

I met Sarah in the parking lot, and we talked just a few minutes as we entered the emergency room. So far, the doctors and nurses were treating Robert for a heart attack. They had given him a shot to thin his blood and were monitoring his heartbeat. They were also concerned about his throat and heartburn. Nothing seemed to help it. Something seemed to be very wrong in his digestive system. Sarah and I stayed at the hospital and waited as the doctors tried to decide what was happening. The monitors showed Robert's heart attack was still in progress long into the night and even to the next morning. Our doctor told us he could not do anything until the heart attack stopped. The enzyme count kept going up continually, showing the heart attack was still in progress. It was too dangerous to do surgery while the heart attack was still going on. Finally, the hospital told us they were admitting him to a room, and they had decided to turn him over to a gastroenterologist. Robert seemed to be having a great deal of distress in his digestive system which they thought was causing the heart problem.

Within thirty minutes of the gastroenterologist coming in and greeting us, we received a message Robert was being taken back to cardiology. They had just received a report back from the Lab. It proved Robert definitely had a heart attack. What a nerve-wracking day! I began to wonder if they were just guessing or sure about anything. I had called on several people to pray for us. I was feeling very numb. I couldn't seem to pull myself together. All I knew was Robert needed God to touch him. God was the only One who knew exactly what was wrong and how to heal it.

Soon, Robert began to throw up big clots of blood. As I stood there looking at him, I knew he was very sick. *How could he live after losing so much blood? Was he going to die only nine months after we had been married? Would God allow this to happen to me, again? Was God allowing this to happen so He could teach me something? Or was this Satan trying to destroy our happiness and cause us to doubt the love of our heavenly Father?* As I prayed, I had the strangest sense of peace that Robert was going to be okay. Even when it looked as if everything was going wrong, I felt peace. I just knew he was going to be all right. I even told family and friends as they gathered to give support and encouragement, "I just feel like Robert is going to be okay." I'm not sure what they thought. They just shook their heads in agreement. Some of them told me they felt the same.

After waiting all day and all night, the cardiologist came in and said he was going to take Robert to surgery. He couldn't wait any longer. He had to know what was happening in order to stop it. It was a risk, but it was a bigger risk to keep waiting. The surgery lasted about an hour. The surgeon came out and announced Robert needed a type of surgery this hospital did not perform. The surgeon was having him sent by ambulance to a hospital about 10 miles away. He would meet us there. He told us not to be concerned if we missed them before surgery. He had called ahead and Robert would be taken straight into surgery the minute he arrived. My children and I hurried to our cars and drove to the new hospital. We arrived just before he was wheeled into the elevator and up to surgery. He looked so white and weak. It was very scary.

For the next hour and a half, we waited and prayed. I still believed he was going to be okay. The surgeon finally came out and announced Robert had one artery that was blocked about 50–70%. He said something had passed through that artery and caused a 99% blockage. It had probably been a blood clot. He said we would be able to see him soon.

As we went in to see Robert in the Critical Care Unit, it was obvious he was very weak. The doctor had solved the heart problem, but Robert was still losing blood very fast. The only solution was to start giving him a blood transfusion right away. The nurse informed Robert he needed to sign paperwork before they could send for blood. He was hesitant about receiving blood, but the nurse told us Robert had lost seven units of blood! He would not live much longer if he didn't receive the new blood. I stood beside him, and we talked about him receiving the blood. Finally, he agreed to receive the blood transfusion. We were just trusting God knew what was happening, and He would take care of him. Even though Robert felt very uncomfortable about getting the blood, he understood he had to do this if he wanted to live.

Even when it looked as if everything was going wrong, I felt peace.

Very soon after this, friends of mine, the Johnsons, came by to see us. They wanted to pray for Robert before they left. As we stood around the bed, Chris told a story of how he almost drowned when he was a little boy. As they were bringing him out of the water, his father was standing on the bank praying. He saw his son wasn't breathing, so he just called out to God, "Father, You know I want my son to live. However, I will accept Your will. If You want to take him home now to be with You, it's okay. I will continue to serve You just the same." As soon as his father stopped praying, Chris started spitting up water and came back to life again. What a story! I wondered what that story might mean to me. I was just too dazed to figure out what it was right then. As we prayed around Robert's bed, we asked God to please heal him and keep him safe.

After everyone left and it was just Robert and me, the nurse started the blood transfusion. As she got it started and walked away, Robert again started throwing up big clots of blood. As weak as he was, it was very hard on him. Plus, he had just come out of heart surgery. I kept thinking, *"What is happening? Am I just imagining Robert is going to be okay? He is very, very sick. The clots of blood are so big! How can he continue to go on like this?"* Then all at once, Robert appeared to not be able to get his breath. He made a terrible sound in his throat, and he raised up in the bed. I literally froze right where I was standing. I couldn't move. I saw everyone around me rushing. I heard them call Code Blue. I saw a crash cart coming in the door. Somehow it all seemed like a dream. I couldn't even pick my feet up to get out of their way.

Finally, I was able to drag myself away from the bedside and shuffle out of the CCU. As I reached the CCU waiting room, I literally fell into a chair. I burst into a heart-wrenching cry to God. "Please, God, don't take Robert away from me. I love him so much, and he makes me so happy. You gave him to me, and he makes my life so complete! I don't want to lose him, but Lord, if this is Your will, I release him to You. Not my will, but Your will be done. No matter what happens, I will continue to love You and serve You." As I finished that prayer, I felt a burden leave me. I realized I had been so afraid of losing Robert I hadn't truly released him to God until that moment. I had to release him to my Lord and be reminded God is always first in my life. He is all I truly need. He is my strength, and He will always be there. I have to trust Him and keep Him first—always. He has to be the love of my life, no matter who else is by my side. I determined to always keep Him first, no matter what. At that moment, I realized God had sent the Johnsons that day to remind me to release Robert to His will. I had prayed the same prayer I had just heard about my friend's father praying over him as he was drowning.

As I finished talking to God, I called my children to tell them what was happening. I got out of my chair and walked toward the CCU door. I looked through the glass just as the gastroenterologist was coming out of the room. He asked me if I was okay. He had been worried about me, but he had to take care of Robert first. I told him I was fine. He said Robert was okay now, and I could see him. Evidently, the new blood they gave him had been a mismatch. He had a reaction to the wrong type blood. It had shut off his windpipe, and he couldn't breathe. The doctor blew oxygen into Robert's airways at a very high rate. He needed to push the oxygen through his windpipe in order for him to be able to breathe again. It was quite a scare, but Robert was finally breathing again.

I was weak from all that had happened. All I could think of was how thankful I was God had saved Robert's life. He could very easily have died with all that was wrong with him: heart attack, internal bleeding, mismatched blood, and then, an oxygen block. I decided to stay by him all night. Mark stayed, too. Soon, the Johnsons came back and prayed the bleeding would stop so the doctors could perform the endoscopy. It seemed once I gave Robert totally to God, he started doing much better. Very soon, we noticed the tube coming from his stomach was not full of blood anymore. The nurse flushed it out because she thought it was clogged, but it wasn't. The bleeding had actually stopped. When the doctor came back that next morning, he was so surprised the bleeding had stopped. He made the nurse flush the tube again, and then he called surgery and took Robert down there forty-five minutes later. He wanted to do the endoscopy as soon as possible, while the bleeding was stopped. I was so glad things were looking up.

My daughter sat with me through the long wait while the doctor explored Robert's stomach. *What could be causing his internal bleeding?* We waited for quite some time as the doctor worked on Robert. Soon, he came out and asked Sarah and me to come with him to a conference room close by. I could tell from the look on his face he did not have good news. As we sat in the room, the doctor showed us pictures of what he had found. Robert had torn his esophagus loose when he was wrenching so hard to get the blood up. Also, the doctor said there was an ulcerated mass between his esophagus and his stomach. The mass had broken open and was bleeding. The mass had probably been caused by acid reflux. He explained this type of cell, when damaged, can easily turn into cancer if not monitored. The esophagus changes after long periods of acid reflux. It becomes damaged and the damaged area turns into what they call Barrett's Esophagus. Robert already had Barrett's Esophagus, which meant his esophagus had been like this for quite some time. The doctor also told us Robert's condition did not look good. He asked that we not mention this to Robert. He had enough problems with his heart. He didn't need to hear the word "Cancer."

The doctor wanted to wait about three weeks, then bring Robert back in and do another endoscopy. This time, he would be prepared to remove the mass and any other cells around it that looked suspicious. As I walked out of the conference room, I couldn't help but wonder what was going to happen to Robert.

Because of the chance of cancer surgery and Robert's condition, I decided to call his family again. I had been in contact with his sister, Rachel. I had promised to let her know if there was any change. I thought his family should know all this new information—just in case. I was really hoping they wouldn't have to come. As Rachel answered, she immediately told me she and Robert's children, Amy and Andrew, and his brother, Richard, were already flying in that evening. They didn't want to wait any longer. They felt they should be there for him.

As the day progressed, Robert became weaker, and the doctor continued to give him more blood. Even though they were giving him blood, his blood count continued to go down. This meant the internal bleeding was still very bad. As evening came, Robert's family arrived from California and Arizona. When they saw him, they became very worried. His daughter burst into tears and ran down the hall. We stayed at the hospital until late that night. Then his family went to our house to sleep.

I stayed at the hospital all night again Saturday night. I wanted to be near him. At one point, I could hear the cardiologist and the gastroenterologist arguing about whether he should have blood thinners. The heart doctor was afraid Robert would get a blood clot since he had just placed a stint in his artery. The gastroenterologist was afraid Robert would bleed to death if he was given blood thinners while he was still bleeding internally. Neither way seemed safe. I just let them argue it out. Finally, the gastroenterologist won the argument and Robert was given no blood thinners. We just prayed it was the right decision. Either way could be fatal.

Even though my nerves were very bad, I continued to feel God was not ready to take Robert home with Him yet. The next day, the doctor came in to tell us he had taken several biopsies in Robert's esophagus. He found no cancer cells. That meant the cancer had not spread. The doctor felt it would be confined to just the mass. That was definitely good news, and we all rejoiced.

However, there was still the problem of the mass. But that day, Robert's blood count started to improve. Finally, we were seeing positive signs. It looked like the bleeding was going to stop.

By Thursday, his blood count was up high enough for him to go home. He had been given eight units of blood but finally didn't need anymore. We were headed home for three weeks of recovery. Robert's brother agreed to stay with us and help. He also wanted to be around when Robert had the final endoscopy to remove the mass on his esophagus. His brother knew how serious that could be. He saw no need to go home and come right back. Of course, Robert didn't know about the upcoming surgery, and we couldn't tell him. He kept wondering why Richard was hanging out with us so long.

As we waited for Robert's endoscopy and surgery, he improved remarkably. In fact, he was feeling so good he was complaining about going back to the hospital for another test. He kept telling us he was fine.

After three weeks, it was time to go back to the hospital. We signed him in and went up to the surgery floor and soon he was in surgery. As I waited, I couldn't help but wonder what God was doing. Robert seemed so healthy now. Surely he was going to be fine. This was so different from the waiting I had done when Stuart was sick. This time, I had confidence Robert was going to be okay. By the time he went into surgery, Richard, and in fact, Robert's whole family, believed he would be okay. He had been through quite an ordeal over the past few weeks and overcome so much. Surely God would continue to heal his body to completeness.

Finally, they rolled Robert back to his room. Then he, too, waited for the results. He became impatient and wanted to just go home. He didn't think we needed to wait for results. After all, it was just a routine checkup to make sure everything was fine. He knew he was fine. Why waste the time? We waited for over an hour before the doctor came into the room. He had such a puzzled look on his face. Again, he brought pictures. The first words out of his mouth were: "There is no cancer." Robert looked at us with a puzzled look on his face. He said, "Cancer? I don't have cancer." The doctor realized Robert hadn't been told about the cancer, so he pulled out the pictures he had with him. He showed Robert what his esophagus had looked like three weeks earlier. Then he showed him what his esophagus looked like that day.

The doctor told Robert he had turned his stomach inside out trying to find the mass that had been there three weeks ago. He couldn't find anything. He said his esophagus and stomach were not only cancer-free, they were in perfect condition! They were as pretty and pink as a child's. There was no sign of any mass *ever* being there. He kept repeating this as if he himself couldn't believe it. He told us he had checked more than once to be sure he was really working on Robert—the same person he had worked on three weeks ago. When he was assured he had the same patient, he gave up. He could give no medical reason why Robert's esophagus and stomach were so healthy. He said it was impossible for him to recover from Barrett's Esophagus in three weeks and for the mass to just disappear with no sign of it ever being there. He kept saying, "I hope you believe in miracles." Then he asked us to come back in three months just to be sure things were the same.

After three months, Robert went back to the hospital for another endoscopy. This time, the doctor checked extra hard to find any sign of a mass. Again, nothing was there. Robert's esophagus and stomach were in perfect condition. The doctor walked in the hospital room to give us the report. He said, "If you don't believe in God, you'd better start believing now. There is no medical way possible for this to have happened!" From that day to this, almost twelve years later, the gastroenterologist calls Robert "My Miracle Patient." He remembers exactly what happened that day, the hospital, the room number and everything about his case. He even tells other people about Robert, "My Miracle Patient." Several years later, my daughter needed an endoscopy/colonoscopy, so she went to see Robert's doctor. When he saw who she was, he immediately said, "Oh, yes, Robert, "My Miracle Patient." And he just had to tell her again all about Robert's miracle healing.

I *know* God healed Robert. I don't know all the reasons why he had to go through his pain and suffering like he did. I do know I recommitted my life and my will to God during that whole episode. I promised to never, ever forget that God is first in my life—now and forever. I will always surrender my will to His. He knows what's best when I don't. He sees the future, and He knows exactly what the desires of my heart are, even if I forget. His greatest joy is for me to love Him with all my heart and commune with Him as friend to friend. My heart truly desires to worship Him and always be found right where He wants me. Whatever I have to go through to keep me close to God is fine with me.

Robert and I continued to serve God and work in our church, so grateful for all He had done for us. Robert decided he wanted to pray for other people to be healed and give his testimony, so he began to do that each week. He saw several people receive complete healing as he became a tool for God's use. He continues to tell his story even today. God was so good to us, how can we be quiet about it?

Then I began to feel God wanted Robert and I to work in the Stewardship Department, helping teach God's principles about money. We signed up to hold a small group at our home and teach a Crown Financial class. We were very surprised to see all the scriptures about money in the Bible and how God teaches us to handle money. I never imagined there were so many biblical teachings on this subject. I probably learned as much as the students. I was so excited to know all of this new information. It truly changed my thinking about money. I had been reading the Bible for years but somehow missed God's teaching on finances. I wanted to teach everyone about our newfound truth.

Chapter 24

Saying Goodbye

About four years later, as I was driving to work one morning, I felt such a heaviness about my job. I loved my job and the people were very good, but somehow things just weren't right. I was getting very tired of the long commute each day. Getting up at 5:15 a.m. every day and getting home at 6:30 p.m. made such a long day. I started crying and praying as I drove to work. Soon I heard myself saying, "God, I know You are releasing me from my job. I don't know where You want me to work. Please, just put my name on someone's heart to call me. Then I'll know I've found the place You want me to work." As I prayed that prayer, I felt a peace come over me. It was as if God was saying, "Okay."

I arrived at work and opened my computer to begin my day's work. As I checked through my emails that morning, I saw an email from a friend who was now working at the church we were attending. I read the email in total amazement. They were asking me if I'd like to work full-time at the church. If I did, I was to send in an application and résumé. They needed someone to do accounting. Even more amazing was that my friend, who had been in a Crown Financial Class Robert and I had taught a year previously, just happened to think of my name and recommend me for the job. He wasn't even working there when he attended our class on finances. He said he remembered me saying I had an hour and a half's commute to work. WOW! How amazing and how quickly that happened! God knew a year ago He'd have me ready to work at my church at this exact time. He was a step ahead of me all the way—He always is!

Of course, I told them I would send in my application and résumé right away. As I told Robert what had happened, he just laughed. All at once I said, "I don't even know what they will pay me." Robert laughed again. "Does it matter? If God has gone this far with it, I think we can trust Him to provide for us no matter what they pay you." I had to agree. I knew God would always provide wherever He led me and this definitely had to be God leading.

It took only a few weeks until I was working right where I knew God wanted me. Getting more sleep in the mornings and being home earlier in the evenings was such a blessing! Plus, I was so happy to work at my own church where I could serve God all day doing what I loved to do best—accounting. I could also watch from a front row seat as my church grew and reached many souls for Christ. Once again, God had me back in full-time ministry. I had just thought I was finished.

During this time, while I worked closer to home, I was also able to spend so much more time with my mother, who was 84 and not very well. My father had just died in 2007, and we were having trouble getting my mother to leave the house. I needed the extra time with her, and I was so glad I had it. Losing my parents was hard, but God was there with me, preparing me for this, just as He has done in every trial of my life. He never fails to bring everything about in His perfect timing. The job at my church was such a blessing to me when my mother needed more care before she passed away in 2011. I was able to take time off when I needed it and then take family medical leave to help with her 'round-the-clock care before she died.

I was so thankful for my husband during this time. My mother became so dependent on him she told me she'd prefer to have Robert staying with her than almost anybody. He understood what she wanted and how to help her. That was a real compliment coming from my mother. Mom asked for Robert to pray with her several times as she settled things with God in her final hours on this earth. I was so glad God placed him there to help Mom—and me. I know God had this all planned years ago. Only He knew the desires and prayers I had prayed for my mother before she died. Again, He gave me the desires of my heart. Mom passed away August 1, 2011. God took her home to be with Him and Dad.

I went back to work two weeks after Mom died, but I soon began to feel like I just couldn't handle the stress of it all. One day, as I sat there wondering if I had come back to work too soon, God spoke very clearly to me. He said,

"Don't worry about it. A year from now you won't be here." Just knowing that helped me to be able to carry my load for just one more year.

I worked for my church for five years before I felt like God was telling me to retire. I was 65 years old, and God was telling me to "rest." It took me a few months to actually realize it was okay to rest. Within a short period of time, I had four different people prophesy to me that God was telling me to enter a season of rest. Retirement and rest wasn't something I understood very well, but I began to seek God and ask Him what He actually wanted me to do. He wanted me to truly rest and trust Him. I am trying to do exactly as He wants each day. Some days, He gives me an assignment, but most days, He wants me to just rest and intercede in prayer for those He lays on my heart. I'm truly enjoying the lack of responsibility and spending time with Him.

As I enter my "retirement" years, and I look back over my life, it is so easy now to see how God was orchestrating my whole life to give me what I desired the most—*HIM.* Even things that seemed to be setbacks or curve balls happened for a good reason. God allowed them to be thrown at me so I would dig deeper and seek after Him more than before. I am so glad I continued to learn and seek God in everything that came my way—good or bad.

Through the years, some people have felt sorry for me when they heard about all the different life crises and problems I have come through, (and I have only shared a small amount of what I experienced) but I feel fortunate. My love for God has increased *so* much, and my joy to serve Him is beyond anything I could have imagined when this journey began.

I can honestly say this has been a *truly wonderful* life. I know now it took God orchestrating all of these life situations to bring me to where I am today. I am totally in love with my Savior and looking forward to the day I meet Him face to face.

As I live out the rest of my years, I hope I can be the influence on my children and grandchildren my grandmother was on me. I want that heritage to live on through many generations and save many souls from Satan's evil schemes in this world. It may be a sin-sick world, but I know God can *and will* keep us centered on Him if that is truly the desire of our heart.

*It is so easy now
to see how God was
orchestrating my
whole life to give
me what I desired
the most—Him.*

What Do I Do Now?

The purpose of my writing this book was to help anyone who reads it to know that God *is* Love and when bad things happen to us, God wants us to choose to lean on Him; let Him walk with us through the storms. We can come out on the other side of every storm unharmed. Jumping ship or caving in is not the answer. It is my desire that everyone who reads this book will receive courage to push through to meet our Savior at *Heaven's Gate*. I would like to give you some things to read or to do that might help you get through your storm(s) and be victorious.

The first thing is to know beyond a shadow of a doubt you have accepted Christ as your personal Savior and Lord. Here is a prayer you may want to pray if you have not given yourself totally to God and made Him the Lord of your life.

Dear God,

I come to You in the name of Jesus. I acknowledge to You that I am a sinner, and I am sorry for my sins and the life I have lived. I need Your forgiveness. I believe Your only begotten Son, Jesus Christ, shed His precious blood on the cross at Calvary and died for my sins. I am now willing to turn from my sin. You said in Your Word in Romans 10:9, that "if we confess with our mouth the Lord Jesus and believe in our hearts that God raised Jesus from the dead, we would be saved." Right now, I confess Jesus as the Lord of my life. With my heart, I believe that God raised Jesus from the dead. This very moment, I accept Jesus Christ as my own personal Savior, and according to His Word, I am now saved. Jesus, transform my life so that I will live to bring glory and honor to You alone, not to myself. I thank You for Your unlimited grace which has saved me from all of my sins. Thank You, Jesus, for dying for me and giving me eternal life.

Amen

Once you have repented of your sins and been totally forgiven of all wrongdoing, you will be totally clean, ready to serve God in any way He wants to use you. You will know you are saved when you can truly say, "He is the Ruler of my life. I give Him total control."

As you go out to live for Christ, you will soon find that being cleansed of sin was only the first step. Your whole life will be different as you begin your walk with God.

Next, you need to be filled with the Holy Spirit's Presence in order to have the power you need to resist the devil when he tries to tempt you or lure you back over to his ways of thinking and behaving. Ask God to come in and fill you completely with His Holy Spirit and give you the strength and power you need to live your life the way He wants you to live it. Ask Him to give you wisdom to recognize Satan's tricks and strength to rebuke any evil that comes your way. Remember to always make God the Ruler of your life and continually ask Him to fill you so full of Him there won't be room for anything else. As He does, you will become more like Him each day you serve Him.

Pray, pray, pray, and read your Bible daily to learn more about God's principles and His character, too. God speaks to us through His Word and gives us direction. During my life, I also discovered that listening to worship music is a very vital key that opens up our hearts to receive what God wants to share with us. Many times, when I didn't know which way to turn, I would listen to worship music, pray and get in His Word. And God would speak to me and let me know which way to go. He impressed strongly on me to do one thing or another. Many, many times, answers came when I was in His Presence.

God will lift you up on His shoulders to walk above the stormy seas and let you walk on the mountains if you will let Him. He will always be there, and you are safe when He is beside you.

Secrets to Surviving the Storms

I found the very best way to combat Satan is to stay as close to God as I possibly can. I must read His Word daily and pray for Him to fill me with His Spirit. As I begin to pray, I have learned that starting my prayers off with praise to God for all He has done and for who He is, opens the door into His Presence. A thankful heart is also a heart that is ready to hear what God wants to say back to it. Remembering all He has done for me and the blessings I have received from Him reminds me of His love for me, and it puts me in a position to truly listen to Him.

I also must make sure there are no open doors for Satan to get in through or that there are no hidden sins in my life. (Things like lies, gossip, jealousy, pride, self-righteousness, lust and pornography are open doors that must be shut.) If I have any of these open doors in my life, Satan will do his best to push them open wider and wider. These open doors will eventually separate me from God. Once these doors are closed, I am in a position to rebuke Satan and recognize him when he does attack me.

Once I have spent time praising God and opening my heart up to Him for correction or anything He wants to say to me, I begin to lay my requests before Him. He will take my burdens and many times show me what to do. Then I end my prayer with praise, thanking Him once more for all He has done and for His Presence, His Love, His Peace, His Joy and for dying on the cross so I could be saved. I thank Him for being my Savior and Lord of my life.

After reading the Word, praising God, checking my heart to be sure I have left no open door for Satan, giving my burdens to Him, then praising and thanking Him for all He has done again, I read the following affirmations out loud. I also read these anytime I feel depression, oppression or anything else that could be Satan attacking me. Sometimes I just read them every morning. It helps me to fight Satan throughout the day. After reading these affirmations with a sincere heart, I read the section where I renounce and remove Satan from me and from around me. This has been a great tool for me in combatting demons. I hope it will be for you, too.

Satan hates to hear how powerful and awesome our God is. He hates to hear about the blood of Jesus which was shed for our sins. He hates to hear about the healing power of God and how all things are possible to those who believe in Him. These affirmations send Satan on the run. He does not want to stay where the name of Jesus is being lifted up and praised.

Daily Affirmations

He brought me up out of the pit of destruction, out of the miry clay, and He sat my feet upon a rock making my footsteps firm.
Psalm 40:2 (NASB)

He put a new song in my mouth, a song of praise to our God.
Psalm 40:3 (NASB)

How blessed is the man who has made the Lord his trust.
Psalm 40:4 (NASB)

Many, O Lord my God, are the wonders which You have done, and Your thoughts toward us; there is none to compare with You.
Psalm 40:5 (NASB)

Then I said, "Behold, I come; in the scroll of the book it is written of me. I delight to do Your will, O my God; Your law is within my heart."
Psalm 40:7–8 (NASB)

Now, I am a living stone, being built up as a spiritual house to offer up spiritual sacrifices, acceptable to God through our Lord Jesus Christ.
(1 Peter 2:5)

I am the righteousness of God in Christ Jesus.
(2 Corinthians 5:21)

Old things have passed away; all things have become new.
2 Corinthians 5:17 (NKJV)

As Jesus Christ is in this world, so am I.
(Romans 8:11; 2 Corinthians 13:5; 1 John 4:4)

I am blessed with all spiritual blessings in the heavenly places in Christ Jesus.
(Ephesians 1:3)

God is my heavenly Father. Jesus Christ is my Lord.
(Galatians 4:7; Acts 16:31; 1 Corinthians 12:3)

He is the image of the invisible God, the firstborn of all creation.
Colossians 1:15 (NASB)

All things have been created through Him and for Him, both visible and invisible.
(Colossians 1:16)

He disarmed the spiritual rulers and authorities. He shamed them publicly by his victory over them on the cross.
Colossians 2:15 (NLT)

God has put all things under the authority of Christ and has made him head over all things for the benefit of the church. And the church is his body; it is made full and complete by Christ, who fills all things everywhere with himself.
Ephesians 1:22–23 (NLT)

He has given me authority to tread upon all the powers of darkness and nothing by any means will harm me.
(Luke 10:19)

I always triumph in the name of Jesus.
(2 Corinthians 2:14)

We are human, but we don't wage war as humans do. We use God's mighty weapons, not worldly weapons, to knock down the strongholds of human reasoning and to destroy false arguments. We destroy every proud obstacle that keeps people from knowing God. We capture their rebellious thoughts and teach them to obey Christ.
2 Corinthians 10:3–5 (NLT)

I take every thought captive to the obedience of Christ Jesus.
(2 Corinthians 10:5)

Through Jesus Christ, I am more than a conqueror.
(Romans 8:37)

I am seated in heavenly places in Christ Jesus.
(Ephesians 2:6)

I have love, joy, peace, patience, kindness, goodness, faithfulness, gentleness, and self-control.
(Galatians 5:22–23)

I take the sword of the Spirit, which is the Word of God, in my mouth, and with it, I destroy the works of the devil.
(Ephesians 6:17; 1 John 3:8)

My Father says His Word will not return void, but will accomplish what He desires, and it will succeed in the matter for which it was sent.
(Isaiah 55:11)

These signs follow me because I am a believer in Christ Jesus. In His name I will cast out demons, lay hands on the sick and they will recover and nothing by any means will harm me.
(Mark 16:17-18)

Say the following declaration out loud:

Right now with the authority given to me by Jesus,
I renounce and remove from me and this room,
all doubt and unbelief, all tiredness and fatigue,
all unforgiveness and all oppression.
I renounce and remove in Jesus' name,
all traditions of men.
I renounce and remove in Jesus' name
all mind-binding spirits.
I renounce and remove in Jesus' name
all sickness and disease.
And now Father, from Your Throne of Grace,
I receive Your Grace, Your Forgiveness,
Your Love, Your Joy, Your Peace
and Your Wisdom.
And in the name of Jesus, I speak peace.

The Lord said, ... "I am watching over my word to perform it."
Jeremiah 1:12

Glory be to God Forever!

www.ingramcontent.com/pod-product-compliance
Lightning Source LLC
LaVergne TN
LVHW021133080426
835509LV00010B/1337